Warkton

A Village in Northamptonshire

Disclaimer

All reasonable steps were taken by the publishers of this book to trace the copyright holders and obtain permission to use the photographs contained herein. However, due to the passage of time certain individuals were untraceable.
The intention of this publication is to portray the village and villagers through a compilation of archival records and people's thoughts and recollections.
Such information is published in good faith and an apology is given for any inaccuracies or omissions which might inadvertently have arisen.

Archives
All the material collected over the years are deposited in St Edmunds Church Warkton.

Local Heritage *initiative*

The Local Heritage Initiative is a partnership between The Heritage Lottery Fund, Nationwide Building Society and The Countryside Agency

Date of Publication: 31st July 2006
ISBN: 0-9553614-0-0
ISBN: 978-0-9553614-0-1
Published by: Warkton Heritage
Copyright © Warkton Heritage

Boughton House
Northamptonshire, NN14 1BJ
Kettering (01536) 82248

June 2006

So many history books seem to bury history. This spirited account brings it to life. It revives happy memories of friends, places and less happy memories of happenings such as floods. As a near neighbour for more than 80 years it is a treat to be able to share in these reminders, even if some were of shock on discovering in St. Edmunds Church that some of my ancestors had apparently been turned to stone! Since then, however, the many characters portrayed - the life blood of Warkton - more than eclipse my negative recollections.

This lively account of life in a truly English village can give pleasure to readers far and wide.

The Duke of Buccleuch & Queensbury, KT

This is a snapshot of the archive material that has been collected by Warkton Heritage's chief Historian Alan Toseland. The composition of this illustrated history was inspired by the people of Warkton. A Heritage Society was formed in 2003 and funding was obtained from The Local Heritage Initiative Fund to facilitate the production of an illustrated history pack for local primary schools and an illustrated book inspired by the immense volume and diversity of Alan's archive materials.

Warkton Village lies within three miles to the east of the centre of Kettering in the County of Northamptonshire. It has just 49 dwellings with a population of approximately 120 adults. The parish of Warkton covers approximately 550 hectares which are currently predominately arable, meadow and in the north woodland.
The casual visitor to Warkton would find it difficult to believe that a village so small could hide within itself such a rich and varied history.

Alan recalls *"the idea of a book concerning Warkton started some 25 years ago, when my father Cyril who, when he was 84 years of age and had lived in the same house, Number 25 Warkton , for all of his life, was asked to record his recollections of the village. He suggested that I perhaps would help him with this task. Together with my wife Pauline I recorded his account of the previous 80 years and beyond. Many of his reminiscences were substantiated by other older folk of Warkton, who also brought to light many other long forgotten incidents. Together with my own generation's memories I started to gather material on the social and historical life of the village, both from searching old records, and by talking to numerous people who were associated in some way with Warkton. Many regrettably are no longer with us".*

Alan owes special thanks to the following:
"I thank wholeheartedly His Grace The Duke of Buccleuch for permission to use material from the Boughton Archives.
The Northampton Record Office and their helpful team of archivists.
The Evening Telegraph Kettering who have given me tremendous help and encouragement.
I especially express my gratitude to three ladies, my wife Pauline and daughter Lindsey who typed the original script, never seeming to get bored with me asking them to type just one more line, and Ursula Jones who assisted with the authorship of the book, typing and retyping many thousands of words to make the book what it is. Without their help it would not have got off the ground.
I owe thanks to Christopher and Edward Lamb both for supporting and helping by adding their family photographs and editing the draft texts.
I sincerely thank all the people who donated their family photographs and stories to add to the narrative of Warkton. I am grateful to all the people mentioned in the book including all the unknown photographers of the past for without them this book would not have been possible.
If I omitted to thank anybody, I apologise. Any errors are entirely unintentional".

Warkton Heritage acknowledges contributions from the following:

His Grace The Duke of Buccleuch and his staff at Boughton House.

The Northamptonshire Record Office Northampton. Sarah Bridges
& Crispin Powell
The Evening Telegraph Kettering. Elizabeth Mc Bride & staff.

Alan and Pauline Toseland and their family
Christopher and Edward Lamb
Ursula Jones
The Local Heritage Initiative
Members of Warkton Heritage

Richard Bussey
Edna Braybrooke
Pamela Denny
Doreen Emm
Mary Hyde
Eileen Irons
David Issitt
Sydney Law
Jennifer Law
The Mutton family
Oliver Nixon
Barabara Sears
Rosalind Tebbutt
Florrie Tilley
John Turner
Gerald & Georgie Worthington

Warkton
A Village in Northamptonshire

Contents

Introduction

The earliest mention of Warkton that has been found is from the year 946, when it was in the hands of King Athelston, a Saxon, at this time he gave it to one of his Thanes or nobleman named Wulfric.

Northamptonshire was invaded by the Danes in 1006, taking the entire county. There are no records to indicate how Warkton was affected by this invasion.

In 1065 Earl Morcar led a Northumbrian army into Northamptonshire and devastated it. Morcar then gave the lands around Warkton to his mother, Aelfeva to hold. Her husband was Earl Algar of East Anglia. It was his mother, Countess Godiva, who reputedly rode on horseback, naked through the streets of Coventry.

At the time of the Norman conquest in 1066, Warkton fell into the hands of William the Conqueror. He gave two Northamptonshire parishes, Scaldwell and Warkton to Bury St Edmunds, for the soul of his Queen, Matilda. This is the reason that the church came to be named St Edmunds.

At the end of the twelfth century, the Abbot of St Edmundsbury, Hugh 1st, conveyed the Manor to Ernald de Herlaw. He, in 1201, conveyed it to Samson de Tottingham, Abbot of St Edmundsbury, for 60 marks (£40), giving an undertaking to burn the charter made to him by the Abbot. (A coin to represent 1 mark or 13s 4d was never minted although many transactions were carried out in marks.)

Warkton was included in a list of Manors appropriated to the cellarers of the Abbey for which custodians were appointed in 1215.

In 1284 the Abbot of St Edmunds held Warkton for the King in chief, and in 1291 he received from it the considerable sum of £22 15s 5 $\frac{1}{4}$ d.

The Abbot was having difficulty with his tenants about rights of common and other matters early in the 14th century. Possibly as a result of these disputes in 1312, he leased the Manor for twelve years at a rent of £80 a year, excepting advowson of the church, (the right of presentation to an ecclesiastical benefice) and Frankpledge. (This was a periodic meeting to see that all men who ought to be were in a tithing. Which is a group of ten householders, mutually responsible for the good behaviour of the group)

The Abbot obtained a grant of free warren in 1330 and proved his claim to view of Frankpledge, in the Manor from time immemorial.

In 1414, when Henry V was King, William Cratefield Abbot of St Edmundsbury, leased the manor for 10 years to Thomas Earl of Dorchester, at a rent of £25 per year. The Earl, in 1417, who had been created Duke of Exeter, wrote to the Abbot, complaining that he had confiscated the lands from his farmer for arrears of rent.

The Abbey continued to hold the Manor until the dissolution, when in 1535 it was in the hands of Thomas Lane for a rent of £32. On 20th March 1541 the Manor and advowson, of the Rectory with all the lands of the Abbey in Warkton, were granted for life. to Sir Edward Montagu, Chief Justice of the King's Bench of Henry VIII, and his heirs. (Sir Edward had already purchased Boughton in 1528).

The Manor and associated lands have remained with the Montagu family to this day, together with the Dukedom, which was created in 1705, when Ralph Montagu was created the 1st Duke by Queen Anne, Ralph died in 1709.

When his son John the 2nd Duke died in 1749 Boughton passed to his daughter Mary, but the title would have lapsed had her husband George, Earl of Cardigan, from nearby Deene, not been created 3rd Duke of Montagu in 1766. Sadly their only son, the Marquis of Monthermer, died four years later at the age of 35.

It was Monthermer's sister Elizabeth who inherited Boughton. She was already married to Henry Scott, 3rd Duke of Buccleuch, and although the Dukedom of Montagu became extinct, the family name continues, combined with that of Scott and, when Duke Henry inherited the Dukedom of Queensberry and that of Douglas, to form, as it is today, "Montagu Douglas Scott".

Since then Boughton has continued as a home of the Dukes of Buccleuch and Queensberry, thereby maintaining the direct family link for over 450 years. The present Duke being the 9th Duke of Buccleuch and the 11th Duke of Queensberry.

The Domesday Book of 1086 gives the following entry for Warkton:

Ipfe abb ten de rege WERCHINTONE. IN NEVESLUND HUND. Ibi funt. iii. hidae 7 dim. Tra. e. ix. car. In dnio funt. ii. car. 7 xvi. uitti 7 viii. bord cu. vii. car. 7 iii. ferui. Ibi molin de. xii. folid. 7xx. ac pti. Silua. Iii. qrent Ig. 7ii. qz lat. Valuit. vii. lib. Modo. vii. lib. Aelueua mat Morcari tenuit.

Translated: we can read

The lands of St Edmunds in Navisland Hundred.
The Abbey itself holds Warkton from the King. 3 ½ hides.
Land for 9 ploughs. In Lordship 2 ploughs;
16 villages and 8 smallholders with 7 ploughs; 3 slaves.
A mill at 12 shillings; meadow, 20 acres; woodland 3 furlongs long and 2 furlongs wide
The value was £7; now £8.
Aelfeva, sic Morcar's mother held it.

A record of a curious incident that happened in Warkton in 1186.
How the Abbot journeyed through the lands of St Edmund, and how he escaped death at Warkton.
The following is taken from a Medieval source book written by Jocelin of Brakelond Chronicler of Bury St Edmunds

After the end of Easter the Abbott went through all his manors and ours and through those which we had confirmed in fee to tenants. And from all and sundry he demanded an aid and recognition, according to the custom of the realm. Daily he grew skilled in earthly learning, and turned his attention to the acquisition of knowledge of external affairs and providing for them.

"When he was come to Warkton and was at night sleeping, a voice came to him saying *Samson arise up quickly*, and again, *Rise, Rise, thou tarriest too long*. So he arose half dazed, and looking round about him saw in a necessary place a light, a candle which Reiner, the monk had left there through carelessness, and which was about to fall on the straw. When the Abbot had put it out, he went through the house and found the door for there was but one so fastened that it could only be opened with a key, and the windows barred. Wherefore, had the fire grown, both he and all they who were sleeping in that building would have perished. For there was no way by which they might have gone out or escaped."

There is ample evidence that the name Warkton came from an old English personal name; Weorc or Weorca. Warkton means "Weorc's Farm"

Warkton has been spelt in many different ways over the centuries, as the following list illustrates.

Werchintons	1086
Whercheton	1166
Wherchtone	
Werkintone	
Werkenetone	
Werkentune	
Werketon	
Werkestone	1233
Werkinton	
Verketon	1248
Warton	1449
Warkyngton	
Warkctone	1689
Werkton	
Warckton	1739

The original medieval village of Warkton was centred around the church. It has always been known that buildings and houses used to stand on sites to the west and north of the church. The last of these were demolished in the 1870s. However, in September 2005, when a gateway that was being constructed at the bottom of the field adjacent to number 6, (opposite the public telephone box) remains of a building were unearthed.

A photograph showing the foundations when they were briefly uncovered in 2005.

Archaeologists from Northampton were called in to examine the find and to survey the area. From shards of pottery that were dug up they found that all the discoveries were from the 12th – 14th century. Nothing later than this date was found at this particular spot. In March 2006, a shard that was found in a neighbouring field next to the Bakehouse, has also been similarly dated.

However in the Rectory grounds two flint arrowheads were found in 1998, these are hollow-based flint arrowheads. The type is well known in Central and Northern Ireland and dates from the late Neolithic/Early Bronze Age. In England and Wales the type is very rare indeed, (0.2% of arrowhead finds). There is then a very real possibility that the arrowheads may have come from some Victorian or Edwardian collection and may not be genuine site finds, though the latter should not entirely be ruled out.

The two Arrow Heads.

A coin and token found by Christopher Lamb in the Playcroft when it was first ploughed by Major Knight in August 1972 to grow chrysanthemums. The coin on the left is a George 1st half-penny dated 1723. The other is a trade token of Thomas Heyricke of Market Harborough, this was worth $^1/_2$d and is dated 1668.

Broken parts of clay pipes are continually being dug up in the village gardens, but at number 8 in 2005 an almost complete one was unearthed, similar to the one in the photograph.

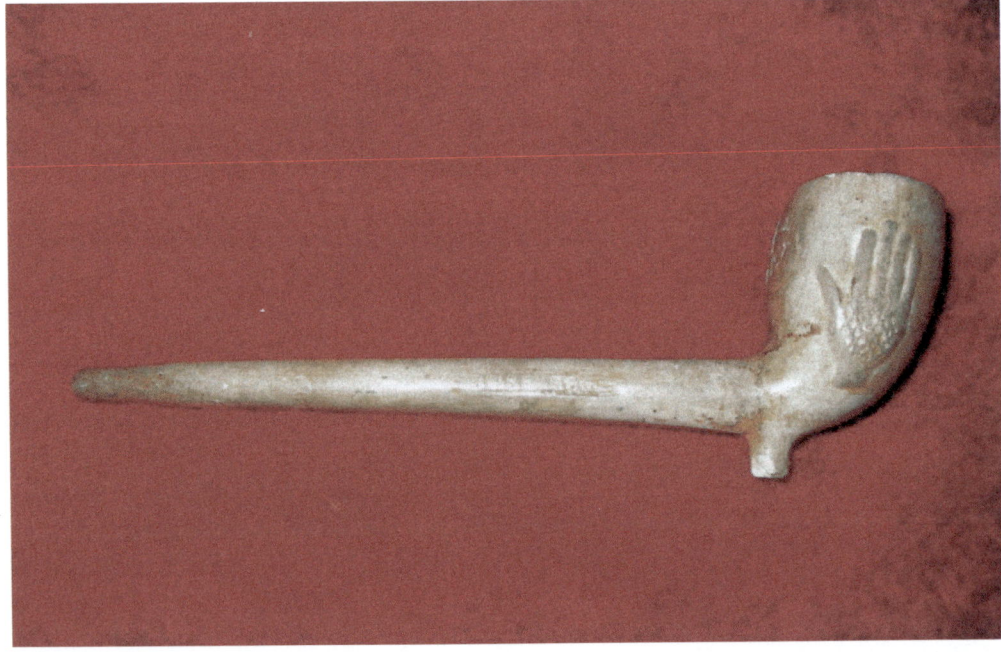

The Black Death reached Northamptonshire in March 1349. The Plague was lethal, killing a victim within five days, and contributed to the disappearance of more than 80 medieval villages in the county. By the winter of 1350, many houses stood empty, and the price of goods fell dramatically. A 40s 0d horse could be bought for 6s 0d and a stone of wool for 9d. The Plague bought bargaining power to the farm labourers, they were in great demand and were able to negotiate a better standard of living. It is not known how or if indeed, the Plague affected Warkton. It is assumed that the inhabitants must have been caught up with this disease one way or another, and this could explain why no pottery shards etc dated later than the 14th century have been found, in this location.

There is a twelfth century document, when King Edward 1 was on the throne, concerning the rights of the Manor of Warkton and Boughton including the names of soldiers and archers. This is written in Latin on a parchment scroll

There seems to have been a flourishing community of tradesmen in the thirteenth century. We have mention of William the Carpenter, who paid a capon for his shop. Richard de Pit for 2 salt pans, 3 capons. Richard the Smith for his smithy, 2 capons. Robert Lee ironmonger 12 d. Richard at the bridge over the Ise, 6d. John Confort who held a messuage near the cross.

Records from the early seventeeth century show rules for Warkton and Weekley Village Feasts, as set out by Thomas Brooke of Great Oakley and Edward Montagu of Boughton House. They were both magistrates and Puritans.

As written in 1615.

No unlicensed beer to be sold
Fiddlers not invited by the villagers, or who play music not pre-arranged with the village leaders to be treated as "rogues"
Any unlawful recreations before the end of Sunday Church Service. Offenders are to be presented and punished "by whipping"
Other invited outsiders are not to linger at the end, but to depart straight away.

Apparently these two villages and indeed others were suspicious of outsiders especially anyone from Kettering which even at that time was a large town by village standards.

The office, Overseer of the Poor was established by the Poor Law Act 1597 and made compulsory by the Poor Relief Act 1601. It superseded the less formal office of Collector for the Poor, which was the first Poor Law Act of 1563. At least two able persons were appointed yearly, at each Vestry Meeting, subject to the approval of the Justices of the Peace. Their role was to levy a Poor Rate and supervise it's distribution. They were unpaid and selected from among the parishioners. A fine of 20s 0d was imposed on any person who refused to act in this post. The collectors accounted for monies each quarter. This continued until 1834 when workhouses were established. After this date Warkton's poor were sent to the workhouse at Kettering, a place to be avoided if at all possible.

The earliest Overseer's account book found to date is 1783, which has the records of the Overseer's levies for turnip accounts, bull monies, and monies collected.

In 1798 John Cave was the Overseer for Warkton and records for that year, include the following entries in the Poor Law Book, called the Town Book.

(Before the year 1798 there were no dates in the Town Book, after this time all entries were dated.)

Paid for a new Town Book	7s 6d
Bought for Marriotts boy 2 new shirts	
a new pare of breaches	
a pare of stockings	
a new pare of shoos	17s 0d
Bought shirts and stockings for Orsbound	13s 0d
Bought shifts and shec for Harriotts when	
had the itch	18s 0d
Paid Dixon the Melishar man	10s 6d
Paid Tom Coles when his wife was ill	2s 0d
Paid for cloath to make Harrotts boy a court	
and making	11s 8d
Paid Thomas Coles to by him and his family	
som shoes	10s 6d
Paid the Overseer of the pour of Harroden for	
letting Thomas Lovell have 42 stone of	
flowers at 9pence a stone under price	£1 13s 0d
Paid Mr Wyment six ginues for a years	
Doctoring the poor of Warkton	£6 6s 0d
Paid for stuff and dressing for the itch	1s 6d
Paid for William Alens wife coffin	10s 0d

By the late Anglo Saxon times in the 10th century, the general pattern of the manorial system was well established in Warkton. The unit of cultivation in the medieval period was called a land, averaging about 8yds x 200yds, or ⅓ acre. In practice there was considerable variation in size. These were ploughed in a clockwise manner which caused them to be ridged up to about 3 ft high in the centre. Lands were ridged up in this way to assist with natural drainage. No hedge, fence or ditches demarcated these strips. Furrows left by the plough were deemed to be a sufficient boundary. Open field farming was a communal affair, and in almost every case, there were no two lands lying together that belonged to the same man. Groups of lands with the furrows running parallel were called furlongs, this referred to an area not a length.

The size of the furlong varied according to the terrain and each had a name. For purposes of crop rotation and the communal grazing of the fallow land, furlongs were grouped together in three large blocks called fields.

On a yearly basis one of these fields would be left fallow, and the others were cultivated. Each of these fields were divided into strips and rented out to farmers, not all of whom came from Warkton. Some farmers rented a number of strips, whilst others had a very small portion.

As there were no fences it was essential for the whole village to arrange and agree a regular programme of crop rotation and fallow grazing, to avoid if possible animals damaging crops. A "Hayward" was in charge of the common herd, with young lads of the village sent to help him, by trying to stop the animals straying from the fallow field. Animals were taken daily from the farmsteads in the village, to the grazing area and back again at night. No separate private herd could be kept, and the dates of hay and corn cutting were regulated, as were the rights of gleaning. There were numerous occasions when disputes arose concerning the tenancy of a particular strip or more often the boundary, when a man had ploughed more than his share.

By the late 1500s, Warkton had three fields of approximately 440 acres each, of ridge and furrow, namely Meadow Field, Moor Field and Wood Field.

The majority of the land in these three fields was owned by the Duke of Montagu. Within each of these three large fields there was a portion of Glebe or Church land. This comprised 8 acres in Wood Field, 11 acres in Meadow Field, 13 acres in Moorfield and 2 acres at the parsonage itself. This land was rented out in the same manner as the Duke's land.

In addition to the above, there were 43 meadow fields lying close to the village of varying acreage from ½ to 8 acres, including one of 15 acres. These were all rented by local farmers who could graze their cows sheep and horses there, and mow some for hay to feed the animals through the winter months.

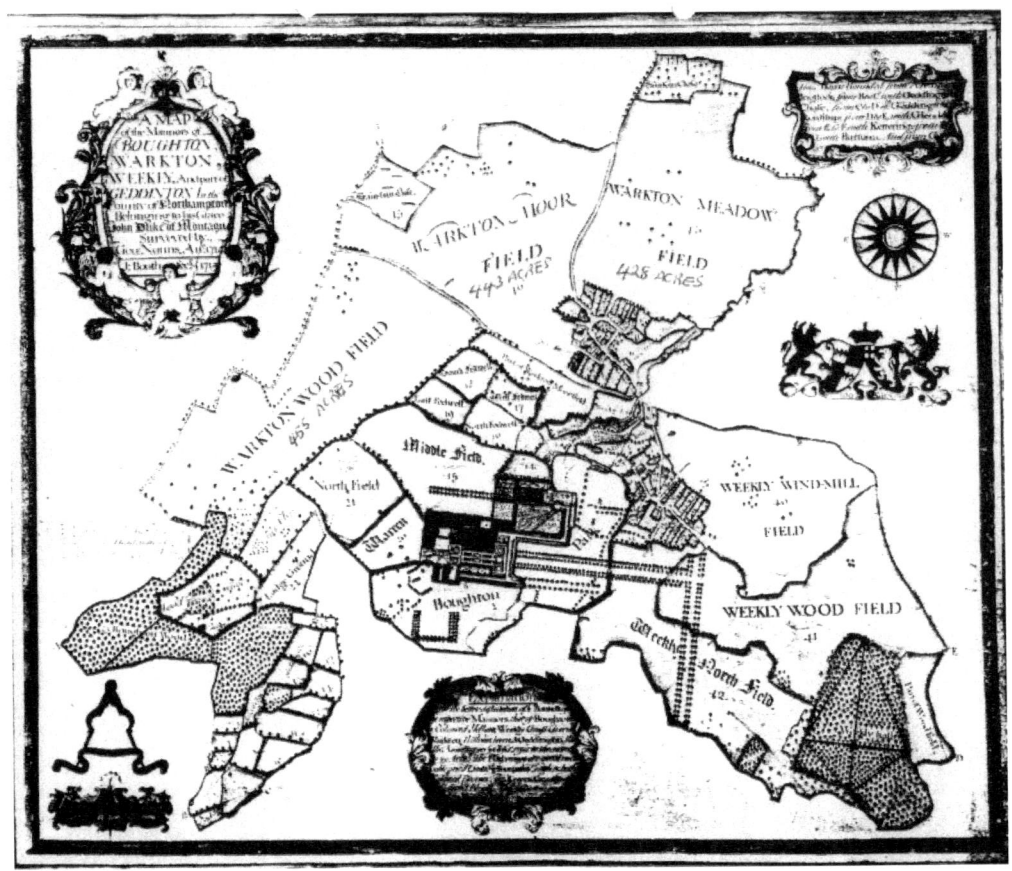

A map dated 1714 showing the three field system

In 1690, 29 Warkton tenants paid £140 14s 8d for their land. The largest by far was Mrs Pitchley who paid £24 6s 3d. The next was John Brampton, he paid £10 10s 0d and Thomas Bird paid just 9d. In this year there was still £61 19s 7d owing from the previous year. In 1717, 8 farmers rented these fields or closes as they were called then.

In addition to the above, there were two areas of about 40 acres each, on the southern border of the parish. One was adjacent to Warkton Lane, the other half a mile further east. These two areas were set aside and planted with Sainfoin (a pink flowered leguminous plant grown for fodder, and good wholesome hay because of it's medicinal properties) in the 16th century to be shared by all the farmers of the village in order to supplement the normal meadow hay that was often in very short supply. These two areas appear on a Boughton Estate map of 1714.

In 1716 there was a dispute between the majority of the farmers and the Estate, in which the Rev Lamotte of Warkton was involved. The farmers were concerned that one man was to be given free Sainfoin without having to participate in it's cultivation.

Eviction was threatened by the Estate and the dispute was resolved with the man in question paying his dues. The Rev said *"this was more to fritten them and oblige them in the future never to dispute it again"*

The ground nearer to Warkton Lane is thought to have ceased to grow Sainfoin when the Lime Tree Avenue was planted in 1745. It is unknown when the other area ceased to supply Sainfoin, but it was probably at the time of enclosure. The lodge that still stands in this agricultural area is now known as Cinquefoil Lodge, and is privately owned.

		1761	A R P
Short Lands	1 Land		0 - 1 - 20
	1 do		0 - 3 8
Long Lands	1 do		1 - 16
	1 do		1 - 37
Holy-do	1 do		0 - 23
Thitmy	1 do		0 - 27
Lee's Piece	1 do		1 - 8
			0 - 27

Wood Field.

Wheat Croft	1 Land		0 - 39
	1 do		1 - 30
	1 do		1 - 0
Jacob's Furlong	1 do		1 - 36
	1 do		1 - 1
	1 do		2 - 38
Old Furlong	1 do		0 - 33
	1 do		1 - 24
	1 do		0 - 37
Acre Lands	1 do		0 - 26
	1 do		1 - 16
	1 do		2 - 17
Pond Furlong	1 do		1 - 12
	1 do		1 - 4
Flax Lands	1 do		0 - 32
Farther new Lands	2 do		2 - 5
Near new Lands	1 do		1 - 0
	2 do		2 - 30
	1 do		1 - 10
Pens Land Slade	1 do		1 - 6
	1 do		1 - 8
	2 do		2 - 29
Clavers Lays	1 do		0 - 32

Warkton Jan: 26. 1761. Jo: Stephenson Rector
Benjamin Clark
Sam. Cave

Glebe Terrier dated 1761. Showing the rents liable to be paid from the tenancy of Wood Field Warkton.

11

Glebe Terrier of 1774
An example of the introduction of the Glebe Terrier for the Parsonage of Warkton.

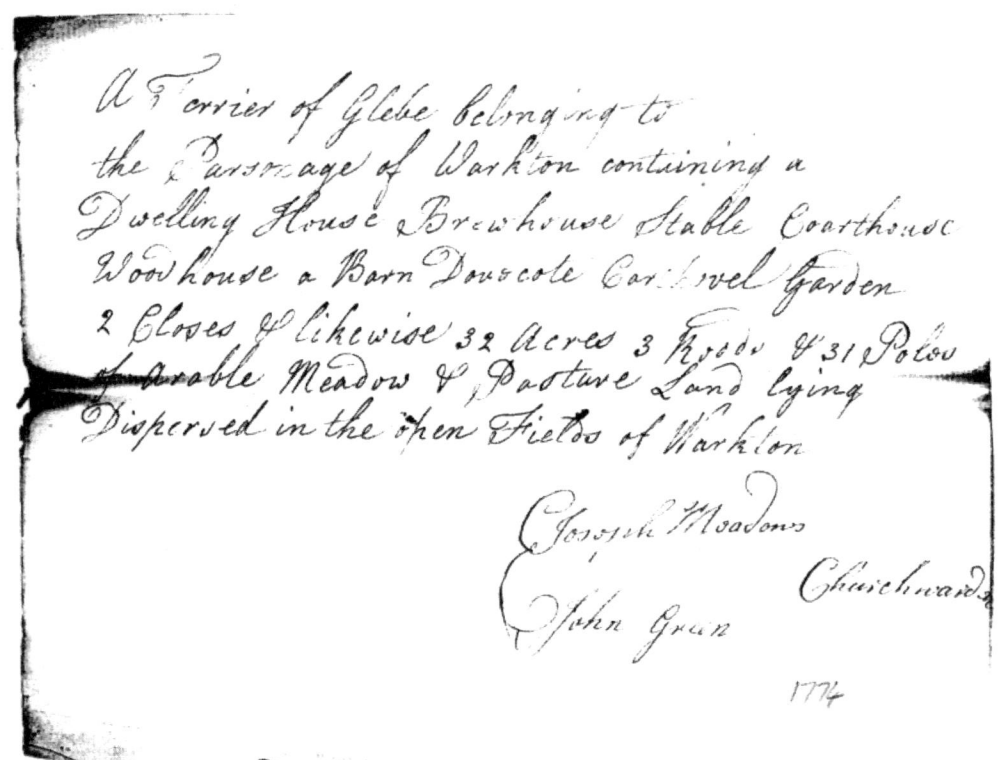

A Terrier of Glebe belonging to
the Parsonage of Warkton containing a
Dwelling House Brewhouse Stable Coarthouse
Woodhouse a Barn Dovecote Cart hovel Garden
2 Closes & likewise 32 Acres 3 Roods & 31 Poles
of arable Meadow & Pasture Land lying
Dispersed in the open Fields of Warkton

Joseph Meadows
Churchwardens
John Green

1774

An 1807 map showing the village before enclosure. Subsequently all the fields were named, most of which are still in use today.

The year 1798 also ties in with the Enclosure Act at least as far as Warkton is concerned. At this date much of England was already enclosed, and Warkton together with Little Oakley were pending for 1807, when the field system would be discontinued. It is assumed that by 1798 the poor of Warkton had already lost their right to common land, which consequently threw them at the mercy of the parish. Before then so long as they could keep a couple of cows and a few sheep along with their gardens, plus a few days work that they could get at hay and harvest time, they could manage to scrape a living, albeit a meagre one. Once they had lost the right to graze their animals they had nowhere to keep and feed them, therefore they had no means of support and the parish would have to do something to alleviate the problem. This is where the Overseer of the poor became involved. Before 1798 there were always some poor folk, for example, the infirm the sick and the elderly, who received certain although very small grants. In most cases these people would have been looked after by their relatives.

The year 1698 was the last year the Poll Tax was exacted. There is a list of Warkton Landowners who were liable for payment. The Tax was paid quarterly at a shilling per head and in some cases children were included.
During this year there was an unusually high number of servants (20) in the village who were also taxed. After 1698 the tax was referred to as the Parish Rate and was calculated on the amount of rent paid annually.

The Parish rate for most years was 3d in the pound, but for the year 1824 it was 6d and again in 1860. This increase in 1824 and 1860 was collected to pay for new church gates and new pathways.
From 1873 it was 1s 3d in the pound which was a huge rise for these tax payers.

Between the years of 1802 and 1809 five houses were built for poor families. These were provided for Emanuel Mutton & Mr Durham in 1802, in 1803 for Mr Busby and in 1808 for Mr Sharp, Mr Coleman had a house in 1809. It was thought that their existing houses had either fallen down, burnt out, become uninhabitable or that they had no other family to look after them. After the houses were handed over to them it appears that they did not receive any poor relief. Other individuals and poor families remained on relief funds. As these houses were built of brick and not the traditional stone, it is assumed that they were in fact attached to the sides of existing dwellings. None of these properties survive in the village to date.

There are records showing the materials used to build these five houses.

An example is:

Expenses at Busby's House	£	s	d
Paid for two loads of wood fetching		12	0
Paid for sawing the wood	1	11	0
Paid for two load of brick and lime fetching		12	0
Paid for six loads of mortar and sand		6	0
Paid Mr Chatte for 1300 bricks & 3 loads of lime	3	6	9
Paid the macenore(mason) & men to serve them	2	11	8
Paid a macenore two days & a man to serve		7	6
Paid ale for the work folks		15	10
Paid carpenters bill for doors windows frames and work	3	8	2
Paid for nails spikes and oiren work for doors and windows	1	4	7½
Paid for lock for door		2	0
Paid for eight bunches of reed		2	8
Paid for two loads of straw	1	19	0
Thacking for same		18	4
Paid Mr Cook's bill for windows	1	9	8
Paid for load of mortar fetching		1	0
Paid macenore and man to serve him		12	6

These five people who received homes had to appear before the justices, and in Mr Busby's case the entry reads:

Attending justices meeting with Thomas Busby and paid for examination	2s	6d
A pair of orders for the removal of Thomas Busby	4s	0d
Going to Wellingborough twice and taking him there	7s	0d

Record dated 1791 showing the charge for thatching a dwelling in Warkton

There are also numerous indictments known as pauper removal, where poor people were claiming poor relief that they were not entitled to, by the fact that they did not belong to Warkton Parish. These people were subsequently sent back to their rightful areas. This of course worked in both ways, where Warkton people were obtaining relief in another parish and were ultimately returned back to Warkton. It was a lengthy and costly procedure, and usually had to go before a court to effect the removal of a family or even a single person, from one place to another. In one case in 1817, the removal of Isaac Allen from Huncote to Warkton involved 45 items of expenditure, including his appeal at Northampton Justices against his removal, which alone cost £27 7s 0d. There was also a system in place where poor men who could do some sort of work, were obliged by law to do so many days labour per year, this was know as "on the round". In 1798 there were 3 Warkton men in this category, John Allen 2 days paid 1s 6d, Tom Coles 2 days 1s 6d and William Harley 29 days paid £1 1s 9d. At the same time persons who paid above £20 in rent, were by law, required to employ a poor man for at least the number of days stated. In 1798 there were 23 people paying levies for poor relief with a total of £47 4s 9d. Over the next fifty years the names were almost always the same both for men on the round and the people paying the poor rate.

The first mention of coal for the poor of Warkton, was in 1807, when a bill was presented to the Overseer for £3 5s 0d for carriage of coal for the poor. This were two years before the canal system reached Market Harborough. When it came it resulted in coal becoming cheaper and more accessible. Thus the 1807 delivery was either collected from Leicester or from the River Nene at Thrapston. In 1809, 11 loads of coal were carried from Market Harborough for the poor of Warkton at a total cost of £18 7s 0d. At a Vestry Meeting in April 1855, it was recommended that *"the charity coals for the poor be bought in the lump sometime in the summer when coal is cheap"*. This coal was stored in a thatched barn near the church to be distributed to the poor in the winter.

Even as late as the early 1900s most of the villagers used to buy goods "on the slate" from the local shop. Charles Spence related how he and others went into Potter's Shop to buy sweets, when Miss Potter was not looking they used to rub their arm against the slate, especially when it was wet, to wipe off the debts.

In the 1890's, Warkton was one of the last villages in the county to be given a specific set of house numbers. Before this, a house was known by the name of the occupant in either Bridge Road or Church Street. By 1911, with houses being demolished and new dwellings being built, this numbering system was no longer comprehensible. It was deemed necessary to start afresh and re-number every house. This number system is still in use today and frequently causes visitors to the village confusion and difficulty in locating their required destination.

An extract from Bridge's Northamptonshire written in 1724, included the following description:

"Warkton named in the Domesday Book Werchenstone seated on the cross of a hill hath Grafton on the east, north Geddington,west Weekley and Kettering and Barton Seagrave on the south. Over the Ise which bounds the west part of this Lordship, is a bridge with five arches repaired according to the cross dividing it by Kettering and Warkton. Here are thirty one houses and one hundred and forty inhabitants. In this Lordship are two quarries, one of soft red stone, chiefly used for foundations and the other to the east of the town a very hard and excellent building stone. In a close which abounds with stone is a petrifying spring. Here was formally found a petrified human skull, sometime since preserved in Sydney College Cambridge. The channel of this spring hardens and fills up so much in time that they are obliged to open a new passage for it. There is also a long deep trench not improperly the remains of Roman works and a coin of the Emperor "Nerva" well preserved has been found in some neighbouring ground. There is a watermill near to Warkton bridge". The bridge was fifty yards nearer to the village than the present one, where the old route of the brook can still be seen.

An extract from Arthur Mee's Northamptonshire, The King's England 1945.

"Warkton. That fine artist Sir Alfred East, who loved to paint the landscapes of his own Northamptonshire, said to his friends "of this fair countryside, that if Warkton village were a hundred miles away they would go to see it."

Though it is not now the great magnificence given to it by Planter John the Second Duke of Montagu, Warkton is still the traveller's delight. It is part of the wonderful estate planned by Ralph Montagu, who developed it in the seventeenth century on the lines of a miniature Versailles. Greatly impressed by the gardens there, which he used to visit as English Ambassador, and being delighted to see the fountains playing in his honour, Ralph the Magnificent, came home and planned his Boughton House, and grounds reaching out to Weekley and Warkton on one side and Grafton Underwood on the other, in the grand manner of Versailles, and his son Planter John followed in his steps. John laid out seventy miles of avenues in parallel rows of elms linking half a dozen villages round".

The Village

This map was commissioned in 1716 by John the second Duke of Montagu as a record of his land holdings for the parish of Warkton. It is one of the earliest known maps that shows the village with many more buildings in place before the existing Grafton road was built, and twenty nine years before the all the avenues were planted in 1745. Prior to the development of the highway to Grafton in the mid eighteenth century, anyone wishing to get to Grafton from Warkton and vice versa with a cart or carriage, had to travel via Geddington or Barton Seagrave and Cranford. People on foot or horseback were able to go across the fields on a narrow track. The map also shows evidence of more built structures around the area of the church, but none visible on the south side. Only eleven cottages can be identified as still standing today. A good number of these buildings were demolished in the 1870s.

It is known that one family that lived in the cottages near the church were the Goodmans, who moved to number forty six when their home was demolished. The parish of Warkton stretches from Barton Seagrave in the south to Brigstock in the north, a distance of three and a half miles, and from the river bridge in the west to Cinquefoil Lodge in the east which is one and a half miles. With the settlement being about one mile east of Kettering, the majority of this parish comprises agricultural land with forestry in the north.

A section from the map on page 20 showing the village in the centre.

This map drawn in 1971 showing ridge and furrow and earth works superimposed on the map.

The surviving earthworks are, in the main, the sites of former houses and associated buildings, situated between and alongside the standing structures.

The remains suggest that the village has not altered in basic layout since at least the early 18th century. An interesting feature is that the earthworks indicate that the present village green was formerly much larger, having been radically reduced in size by encroachments.

WARKTON   Settlement remains

WARKTON

Scale of feet

This map shows the village layout from the bridge on the west to the Grafton Road in the east.

There were two railways proposed for this area of the county, and had they come to fruition, would have passed through, or very close to Warkton parish. The first, Northampton, Lincoln and Hull railway, would have had stations at Kettering Weekley and Geddington. It was surveyed in 1884 and placed before Parliament in November 1845, but the Act was not passed. This was twelve years before any railway came to Kettering, when in 1857 the Leicester to Hitchin line was built. In 1882 another line was proposed, but not put before parliament, for the London and North Western railway to have an end on junction with the existing Higham Ferrers branch line which terminated there. The new proposed line to Kettering was to have been via Irthlingborough and Burton Latimer and then on to Rugby with a station at Rothwell. This line was considered once again in 1898 but nothing further was done. Even as late as 1923 a line was suggested to run from Rugby to Peterborough via Kettering which would of necessity have passed through the parish, but was dismissed on cost.

Warkton viewed from Weekley in 2002. Showing the meadows between Warkton and the edge of Kettering.

Pony and trap at the edge of the village 1911. This is believed to be Dr Roughton. Warkton meadows are seen in the background.

1910 Summer time in Warkton. Mr Mutton with the hay cart in the first field over the brook towards Kettering. He had a smallholding at number 31.

WARKTON VILLAGE, NEAR KETTERING.

B 10541

Weekley Mill in 1895. Although just over the border in Weekley Parish it figured a lot in Warkton's history. Old men of the village used to talk of taking corn to be ground there. It ceased working in the early 1890s and was demolished in 1910. It was worked for many years by the Ward family. The last person to grind corn there was Charles Ward, who married Elizabeth Panther whose family worked the Tannery. After 1864, the mill was run with the use of a steam engine, when the water levels were low.

August 1912. showing the three Folly cottages, as they were known, that were demolished in 1921, due to their continual dampness and frequent floodings. These cottages were situated on the Weekley side of the bridge.

Forty years since flood at Warkton

ANXIETY among some local farm workers was growing towards the end of last week, as the rain continued to fall, and must have reminded some of the older hands of a similar period just 40 years ago this week, when, after a dry July, torrential rain fell for several days.

John Tyler, at 78, claims to be one of Warkton's oldest inhabitants, and remembers well the deep floods which poured down the village roads and swamped the hollow of this picturesque hamlet to a depth of six feet in places, making farming impossible, rotting tons of potatoes, and isolating the village from the main road.

The brook, which this week is being used by children on holiday for paddling and catching tiny fish, became a roaring river overnight as water swept down the fields from Weekley and Warkton Lane, and swelled its banks until every roadside ditch was filled and the road transformed into a lake.

Marshy fields

Traffic coming to Kettering from Grafton Underwood had to be diverted along the "top road" and into the town through Barton Seagrave, while most pedestrians wishing to get to Weekley made their way through marshy fields to come out behind the village.

On about August 12th, the rains stopped, but it was some time before the water subsided, and Mr. Tyler, who was working in Weekley at that time, rather than take the field route, braved the floods night and morning to journey to and from work.

He recalls coming home one night and, on entering the water, soon found it licking round his knees. As he went on it reached his waist, and in parts was up to his chest.

Two cottages which once stood in this hollow, but which have now been demolished, were flooded on the ground floor, and entrance to the houses was only possible through pantry windows fairly high up at the rear of the buildings.

Horse and cart

If any villagers wished, they could get a horse and cart to take them across the water, but this service was not always available.

Of course, to the children it was all a gay adventure, and many availed themselves of the new "swimming pool" which had sprung up on their doorsteps.

When it was again possible to get on the land, Mr. Tyler dug his potatoes. The earth came up in slimy, heavy clods, and his crops were rotten.

But a man of his years has learned to know the weather, and he does not foresee a similar catastrophe this year, and is taking advantage of the sunny weather to tend his allotment, which now keeps him occupied during his retirement.

The floods as reported in the Local newspaper

28

Folly cottages. Although technically just in the parish of Weekley, they were always known as Warkton cottages, and their inhabitants considered themselves Warkton parishioners, attending the church and any other village functions. This shows their close proximity to the bridge and its' associated flooding problems. The house next to the road shows Mrs Coleman who used to sell mineral waters. The gardens and privies to these houses, were the other side of the bridle path that led to Weekley. The gardens were still in use by men from the village as allotments in the 1940s. Now there is no visible evidence of either the homes or the allotments.

Folly cottages drawn
in 1890 by George Harrison,
a well known local artist
who lived in Kettering.

This picture shows part of the rear of the Folly
Cottages and the bridge, looking towards Warkton,
taken from the Weekley bridle path C1910.

A motor car in floods at the bridge in 1904. This was one of the earliest motor cars in Kettering, believed to be owned by Dr Lee.

A Flood Reflection.

A striking photograph taken during last week's floods at Warkton. For a time the road was well-nigh impassable.

A bus in the floods at the bridge in September 1927. When the river Ise was in flood the village was cut off from Kettering. The route to be taken in this event was via Barton Seagrave.

WARKTON PLANK. A lorry delivering firewood bravely plunges through the water.

A lorry delivering firewood to the villages struggling through more floods at the bridge in January 1928.

A lorry in floods in May 1932. This lorry was loaded with eggs, the photograph was used in a widely distributed advertisement saying "we collect your eggs whatever the weather".

Easter floods in 1999, showing a car and a delivery van navigating the flood water. The flooding problem is still evident when exceptional storms hit the County.

The old road bridge in 1890. Edwin Mutton is with the horse.

The first account of a bridge at this point is in 1689. In 1725 there is a record that states that the bridge had six arches with a cross in the middle dividing the parishes of Kettering and Warkton. This was believed to be fifty metres nearer to the village than the current bridge. This theory was substantiated, when in 1901 some digging revealed a line of wooden posts situated at both sides of the road, indicating the position of the original bridge. It is still possible to follow the old line of the brook in the field adjacent to house number one.

An inventory dated 1787 records road mending equipment, branding irons and fire rakes (used for pulling burning thatch off houses). "There was belonging to the Town of Warkton a great and little stone hammer, a stone rake, and a peckatt (a pickaxe) for the highways, a town brand which always hangs at the blacksmiths. A town iron bar was to be found at Joseph Meadows." A fire rake, to be used in the village, hung at number 46 for many years.

The bridge after the 1901 alterations. The bridge was raised in height, using the pillars of the old bridge, to try to eliminate future flooding  problems, by allowing more water to pass underneath. Unfortunately this did not have the desired outcome.

The dates and boundary marker in the "new" bridge. On the north side of the bridge the parish boundary is Weekley and Warkton. On the south side, as can be seen, the boundary is Kettering and Warkton.

Further attempts to stop flooding problems resulted in the road to the west of the bridge being raised in height in 1936.

WARKTON FOOTBRIDGE'S LAST DAYS.

Having raised the height of the road, the footbridge known as "the Warkton plank" was removed in 1936.

(left)
Road traffic accident 1995. Over the years there have been numerous accidents over this narrow bridge, including a serious one during the second World War, when a bus carrying American service personnel from Grafton air base, fell into the river causing many injuries.

(below)
A new footbridge was built across the river in April 1970 because it was becoming increasingly dangerous for pedestrians to walk across the bridge with the increase motorised traffic.

A painting in 1874, showing the Roman bridge which was located some quarter of a mile south of the current village bridge over the Ise. The Roman bridge collapsed in the early 1970s and was never rebuilt.

THE photographer was a mile from the village of Warkton when he took this first day of spring picture of Warkton. He used the "Evening Telegraph's" new "Long Tom" lens and his vantage point was near the site of the Grange Farm on the Stamford Road.

The photographer was a mile from Warkton when he took this picture on the first day of spring in March 1951, using the Evening Telegraph's new "Long Tom" lens. He was standing on the Stamford Road near Grange Farm, which has long since been demolished.

A winter
view of
Warkton
meadows
along the
Ise C1920
looking
towards
the village.

Another view of Warkton taken twelve years later, from the west side of the Ise, in
January 1932.

1932. A photograph of the watermill that was situated where
Deeble Road now crosses the Ise.

A painting of the watermill in 1930 showing the footpaths and fields, where the
Ise Lodge Estate was developed in the 1960s.

A painting of the rear of the watermill, in 1915.

A footbridge situated where the watermill used to be 1932. The bridge was built as a result of an accident that occurred to a young child who, whilst playing near the brook, fell in and drowned. Before this the only way across the river was by a precarious bridge that only the miller had the right to use to access his fields. Kettering Rural District Council erected this footbridge thus creating a public footpath through to Warkton Lane.

The rear view of Moorfield Farm cottage. This was originally the Manor Farm, and was rented by the Panther family for almost two hundred and fifty years. The Panthers were farmers and tanners.

The tannery which was sited to the rear of Moorfield Farm. The tannery was built in the early 1700s and was in continual use until the late 1880s in the ownership of the Panther family. As well as the tannery, they lived and farmed what was then called Manor Farm. In 1865 the heaps of oak bark, stored outside and used in the tanning process was deliberately set alight by men who were opposed to the introduction of mechanisation. According to newspaper reports, the fires could be seen for many miles.

The picture shows Mr Hedley Lomas's new milking parlour which was built in 1948.

The village fish ponds. These were originally used to farm fish for consumption in the winter months when meat and eggs were not available. The village constable had to ensure that it was used properly and equitably. These fish ponds were situated adjacent to the tannery.

A picture showing all that was left of the tannery in 1990. Today there is no visible evidence of the tannery . Water that was essential for the tanning process was drawn from the fish ponds above the tannery.

Although the plant was located near the River Ise, there was no means of pumping water up to the site.

1914 This shows the wash pit in the River Ise where the village farmers came to dip their sheep twice a year. This was compulsory. Farmers from Grafton Underwood, Weekley and the north side of Kettering also used this pit. After the First World War farmers gradually built their own sheep dips, consequently this was no longer needed.

This view shows the road into the village from Kettering in April 1920.

This picture C1920, shows number 1 and 2 Warkton with number 3 further up the road. Number 3 was demolished in 1968, because it was built at such an angle into the road that it was increasingly causing dangerous traffic incidents as the numbers of motor vehicles increased through the village. During the Second World War an army tank was driving through the village and knocked the road side corner of the cottage right out. In 1942 a cyclist was killed as a result of his collision with the corner of the cottage. In 1944 a vehicle transporting two wings for a Flying Fortress, up to Grafton Aerodrome, became jammed between the cottage and the wall opposite. The road had to be closed for two days while the wings were lifted and removed by two large cranes. Luckily the cottage and the wall were not too badly damaged by this incident.

Number 3
Warkton being
demolished in
August 1968
to make the
road wider and
safer for the
increasing flow
of motorised
traffic through
the village.

Numbers 1, 2, 3 & 4 Warkton in December 1928
These cottages as late as 1910 had no indoor staircase fitted. In order to access the
upper floor of these cottages, it was necessary to climb up an outside ladder that
was fixed adjacent to an upper door.

Warkton, near Kettering

This shows numbers 1, 2 and 3 Warkton and The Firs farm house on the left 1920. (Now called Moorfield Farm) This was originally the Manor House that was renamed The Firs due to the close proximity of two Fir trees. The Manor House was occupied by the Panther family from the early 1700s until 1893.

The new bathrooms added to the rears of numbers 1 & 2 in 1948. Prior to this there were only five flush lavatories in the village. Villagers used their own privy in their gardens. In 1947 the government decreed that flush lavatories and bathroom facilities should be provided in all dwellings. Thus Warkton had these facilities added, many had to have a small extension built in order to accommodate a bathroom and lavatory.

Two ladies, Mrs Eastbrook and her Aunt Sarah C1890 outside number 5. This house in the early 1900s until 1950 was the village shop, where confectionary and small sundry items were for sale. Mrs Owen and then her daughter Hilda were the proprietors from 1908 until it closed in the 1960s.

This sketch was printed in the London Daily Graphic in June 1872.
It illustrated the life of agricultural labourers and how they
lived. The sketch shows Warkton from the lower end of the
village looking towards Kettering.

This sketch was also printed in the Daily Graphic in June 1872.
It shows old and new cottages in Warkton. Showing the Bakehouse and
new cottages behind.

1999 picture
showing the
Bakehouse and
the new cottages.
In 125 years
there is little
difference to be
seen from the
exterior of
the buildings.

This shows the Bakehouse on the left, looking towards number 46. The Bakehouse was built in 1621 and was used to supply bread to the village. The baker was permitted to ring the oven bell (from the church) to signify that the baking oven was up to temperature, and thus the villagers could bring their Sunday food to be cooked in the oven.Warkton and Kilsby were the only two villages in Northamptonshire that were permitted to use the oven bell in this manner. By the 1920s bread was baked in Kettering and delivered to the village by the baker's boy on his bicycle. The loaves were carried in a large basket attached to the front handlebars. These deliveries occurred three times a week.

The south side of the Bakehouse showing the location of the bakers' oven, which was still in situ in 2000. A new roof for the oven area was constructed in 2005.

The original Blacksmith's shop was located opposite the Bakehouse. This picture also illustrates the primitive lavatory arrangements from the 1600s. It is possible to identify the privy for the Bakehouse and the Blacksmith's, it is the small building with the grey slate roof. This privy was a soil pit type which had to be manually dug out and "resoiled" on a regular basis, it was still in use in the 1940s.

To the right of the Bakehouse was the Village Pound. This photograph shows all that remains in the 1990s. Any animals that were found wandering from Warkton Common were brought to the village and impounded until their owners could pay the Village Constable for their release. Fines varied according to the type of animal impounded and the length of their stay. Frequently, villagers could not afford the fines and in these circumstances, the Village Constable would see that the animal concerned was rehoused on The Estate. This procedure carried on in Warkton until the application of The Enclosure Act in 1807.

After 1807, when the pound was no longer in use, the building was taken over by the parish church for use as storage for the bier and coffin boards etc used for village funerals. This is also the area that was used for the storage of coke for the church heating, which when required was taken in a wheelbarrow to the boiler in the centre aisle of the church. Up to six loads were needed for just one Sunday's heating.

1903 The rear of Isebrook Farm house, showing Thomas Turner, his wife, and their first child Thomas. The small cottage attached to the farmhouse, on the right hand side, was demolished in 1904. It had very low doorways and ceilings and was in a very poor state of repair. Just before this cottage was demolished, Mrs Edith Toseland, local midwife, was called to the cottage to assist with a childbirth, when she misjudged the height of the doorway and had to be taken by horse and trap to the hospital at Kettering with a badly cut forehead.

At this time the farmhouse was renovated, resulting in a new front door being erected, and thus the rear became the front aspect. This is illustrated in the second picture.

Number 25 in 1910 with Edith Toseland in the garden. This was the end cottage of six commonly called "six row". In this year number 24 was joined with number 25 to make one larger cottage. Notice the old doors and windows, these were eventually replaced in 1956.

Rear of cottages 20 to 25 in the winter of 1974.
In the 1850s, records show that these six cottages and the four cottages further up the road, between them housed forty five children and their parents. These ten dwellings were built in the 1820s to provide inexpensive housing for farm labourers, and each had one room upstairs and one down, with the lavatories outside. In the 1870s the cottages were renovated to include a kitchen/wash house on the rear of each property, and the bedrooms were partitioned into two rooms to provide privacy.

Number 33 in 1927, taken from the bedroom window of number 20. On the right of the picture is a radio mast that was erected in order to receive radio signals. These were to be found in most cottage gardens at this time.

Similar to the previous picture, but taken in the winter of 1927.

This picture taken in 1933 shows number 33 on the right.
This cottage also served as a village shop until the 1920s. Showing the bay
window which was added when the shop was first opened, to display the goods
for sale.

Cottages number 32 on the left and numbers 39 and 40 on the right, in
the 1890s. Number 39 was built in the late 1700s, by a villager in his
spare time, he was an employee of Boughton Estate. As with some other
dwellings the ceilings both upstairs and down were so low that it was not
possible for an adult to stand upright. Additional height was only gained
by excavating the ground floor inside area in these types of dwellings.
This cottage was used as a base for Home Guard training in the Second
World War and was demolished in 1946 due to it's poor state of repair.

The Club House taken in 1980. The club was opened in 1913, when number 12 ceased to sell beer. This building was situated directly behind number 32, and was formerly used by the blacksmith to accommodate his horses on the ground floor, and his ironwork above. The club was opened and run by Mr and Mrs Cope who lived across the road at number 37. Apart from Mrs Cope who acted as barmaid it was male only club, originally it was only open for men who lived in Warkton or Weekley and those men who worked on the Estate. The club closed in the 1960s after having run successfully for approximately fifty years.

The Village Green in the 1920s. Ancient records show that the village green covered a much larger area than the current size. The elm tree on the right was felled in 1955 due to its increasingly dangerous condition.

1921. This house, number 31, was the village pub until 1874, The Duke's Arms. The pub closed as the result of a tragic incident involving a baby left outside the premises in a pram.

WARKTON.

Coming down the hill from Grafton Underwood in 1950, showing the Village Green with number 40 on the left and the threshing barn on the right. This is where the villagers were able to get their gleanings threshed. During the harvest, villagers were allowed to glean any corn that was left lying in the fields after the last stook had been removed.

The front view of the threshing barn can be seen on the left of this photograph. Taken in 1958 from the field between the Lime Avenue and village.

These two cottages were built in the 1870s by The Reverend Stobart one to be used for his gardener, and the other for his coachman. These cottages were built using mainly flint as opposed to local stone, because the Reverend came from Norfolk where this style was the norm. These cottages were on the edge of the Rectory land.

66

The Rectory in 1929, built in about 1860 and extended in the 1880's (architect Benjamin Ferrey) to replace the former Parsonage, which was situated in the gardens, to the rear of this building, adjacent to number 43. The Rectory gardens were developed by the men of the village, who were required to give their time and skills to this task at the end of their working day, over a period of four or five years.

Number 45. Taken in the 1920s. The Fletcher family lived here from 1809 to 1933. This cottage is larger than the majority of family dwellings in the village.

The surrounding land was cultivated for vegetables which were used by the family as their staple diet. Self sufficiency was practised by all the families in the village at this time. In 1933 the Toseland family moved in and it became the farmhouse for the family farm.

Number 46 taken in the 1930s with Lewis Goodman leaning on the gate. Prior to 1830, this was a smallholding which comprised the right hand side of the cottage only. The cottage was extended to its current size with a brick building to accommodate a butchers shop. The Bagshaw family from Grafton Underwood moved to Warkton to run the butchers shop. In 1833 Mr Bagshaw attended a sale at The George Hotel Kettering and bought three silk hats for 2s 6d.

1995 this shows number 46 with a new thatched roof and a flower garden.

Number 12. This was built in the early 1800s occupied by a family who developed part of this house into a commercial laundry.

When this laundry facility closed in the late 1880s, some of the villagers built small wash houses in their gardens. Here they installed a fireplace with a copper basin above, where water could be heated and thus clothes washed. Traditionally this washing procedure was undertaken on a Monday. Clothes were dried either on an outdoor clothes line or if wet on a clotheshorse placed in front of the living room fire. On a Friday evening the copper was once again lit to provide hot water for the family bath time. This took place in front of the living room fire, in the winter months, in a tin or galvanised oval bath tub placed on the floor.

Until mains water was supplied to the village in the 1930s, there were six public water taps, positioned around the village where villages went to collect their water. Prior to this every house had a water well, water was obtained using a rope and bucket.

Number 12 had a well situated in the front garden which was used for many years until in 1885 when the whole family fell ill with an infection whose source was traced to this well. It was discovered that the spring feeding this well came from the churchyard and was contaminated.

When the village pub closed in 1874, beer was sold from this house but no licence was given for the consumption of beer on the premises.

A view taken from the church tower in 1985, showing the thatched cottage number 46 on the right. The tiled row of cottages, numbers 8 to 11, were built in 1827 as a better type of labourers' cottage. They were built from stone with tiled roofs, and each had two bedrooms upstairs and a separate kitchen, pantry and living room downstairs. Outside they had their own wash house and privy. The long gardens gave ample space for the cultivation of vegetables.

The house on the left, number 7 was a smallholding with approximately two acres of land.

The Church

A photograph of St Edmunds Church which is a grade one listed building,
taken in 2005.

For over one thousand years a church has stood on this site. Although it is
not possible to see them now, traces of Anglo-Saxon work have been
discovered in the fabric of the church. In 1867 part of a small Anglo-Saxon
clerestory window was discovered over the eastern most arch of the south arcade,
but it was then replastered. This seems to point to an Anglo-Saxon church which was
subsequently altered in Norman times.

The arches which can be seen on each side of the nave are early Norman work. The
columns are quite plain with square, lipped capitals and simple pediments.
The arches themselves were probably chamfered smooth at the time of the general
alterations made in 1748.

The tower, the aisles, the chancel and windows of the church differ considerably
from the Norman work of the nave arcades. The tower seen from the outside is a
very superior example of the perpendicular style both in design and proportion. It is
dated C1420/1450.

Behind a small door there is a stone spiral staircase with sixty steps leading up to
the belfry, with a ladder reaching to a further eight steps leading to a trap door to get
out onto the roof. Some of these steps were renewed forty years ago, as they were
very dangerous, almost worn completely away by the centuries of people climbing
up to the bell chamber.

Out on the roof, carved on the lead are sixteen legible names and dates from the
earliest 1681 to 1881, many more are weather worn and are unreadable.

It is reasonable to suppose that the Norman nave extended eastwards into a Norman chancel arch and chancel. It is known that in the thirteenth century a chancel and arch were built in the Early English Style. But the chancel arch that is to be seen today is a reproduction of the Early English arch, found there in the alterations of 1748. These alterations were carried out by John the 2nd Duke of Montagu, who entirely rebuilt the chancel and generally redesigned the church.

Duke John's aim was to provide a memorial chancel for his family. His father Ralph, the 1st Duke of Montagu, who died in 1709, had already created a tomb house in the north aisle, and is buried there. When Duke John rebuilt the chancel in the Palladian style, in 1748, he enlarged this tomb house, built niches in the walls of the chancel to house family monuments, and almost completely blocked up the old chancel arch by building a wall against it. Entrance to the chancel was through a small arch above the chancel steps.

There are four monuments in the chancel:

John 2nd Duke of Montagu 1749 by Roubiliac.
John 2nd Duke of Montagu died in 1749 he had married Mary Churchill the daughter of the 1st Duke of Marlborough, the "afflicted widow" who erected this monument and appears on it. The figure of the boy on the ledge is hanging up the oval medallion displaying the profile of the Duke. On the right stands Charity with two children, her arm stretched up to help him. The standing child is weeping and holding in his right hand the symbol of an extinguished torch. On the left is the figure of the Duchess, with his coronet and shield of arms. To the left of her are military symbols – a gun barrel, cannon balls, a flag, and a trumpet representing Fame.

Mary Duchess of Montagu
1751, wife of John,
by Roubiliac
The Duchess died aged sixty
one, and this monument "in
pious remembrance of the
best of mothers" was erected
by her daughter Mary,
Countess of Cardigan, later
to become Duchess of
Montagu. The three figures
are those of the three Fates.

Mary Duchess of
Montagu 1775,
wife of George
Brudenell 4th
Earl of Cardigan
created the 3rd
Duke of
Montagu.
Designed by
Robert Adam,
the Scottish
architect, with
sculpture by
P.M.van Gelder.
The Duchess is
expiring on the
right, whilst an angel on the left gestures towards heaven. The grieving child
points to her coronet.

GROUP OF STATUARY, WARKTON CHURCH, NR. KETTERING.

Elizabeth Montagu, wife of Henry, 3rd Duke of Buccleuch 1827 by Thomas Campbell.
The angel on the right is holding in his hand the symbol of an extinguished torch.

There are twenty two members of the Montagu family interred in the family vault including six children, with name plates on each lead coffin. The first was placed there in 1702 and the last in 1844. Prior to 1702 the Montagus were buried in Weekley church.

In 1748 all the windows in the church were reconstructed with the exception of the tower windows and the window in the south aisle which was bricked up. Duke John also erected box pews, a triple decker pulpit, and built a musicians gallery against the tower arch. For some unexplained reason he replaced the font bowl and discarded the original vessel which the local blacksmith used for many years as a water trough where he cooled his iron work, horse shoes etc after they had been heated for bending and shaping. At some point in the mid nineteenth century, probably when the blacksmith's shop was moved to the other side of the village, the medieval vessel was cast aside and placed in a field to be used as a drinking trough for cattle and horses. John Harris, blacksmith, disclosed that he had taken over the font amongst the effects of the village smithy in 1816, and that it had been there in the occupancies of Mr Waters and Mr Braines his predecessors in the smithy.

At a Vestry Meeting, held in the old school room on the 17th August 1867, at 3pm, the inhabitants of Warkton were invited to attend to discuss and approve the proposed alterations and to determine the sum of money to be spent. They agreed that £500 be spent on the improvements. As this took place in the afternoon only 13 people attended, which included the very energetic Rector of the day, the Rev Henry Stobart, who was involved in the church restoration, leaving the church very much as it is seen today.

The box pews, the old pulpit, the gallery and the wrought iron work that had surrounded the monuments were all removed, and the present pulpit was erected. The floor of the nave and the aisles was lowered and repaved. The font bowl of pre 1752 was taken from the field and replaced in the church on a new pedestal. The bowl that was taken out was abandoned in a corner of the churchyard, where it remained for forty years. It then found it's way into a nearby garden to be used as a flower container, and is still in use in that role today.

The Rev Stobart opened up the chancel by removing the wall erected in 1748. Thus the old 13th century arch was discovered, badly twisted and decayed. The present arch was constructed as a replica of the original.

This shows the church font in 2006.

In 1865 the Rev Stobart produced an Almanac which he had printed for all the regular church congregation. It included a record of births, marriages and deaths for the preceding year, and notable national and local events, abnormal weather conditions, and a daily bible tract. The Almanac was well received by the congregation, so much so that it became an annual publication until he left the village in 1883.

He often mentioned the fact that there were too many illegitimate children being born in the village, especially so in 1869, when out of eighteen babies born five were out of wedlock.

His successor the Rev Coulson Bridges, continued the publication after his first year at St Edmunds. He produced a yearly Almanac, with the exception of one volume, on the occasion of his wife's death, until he moved away in 1909. There were forty of these produced in total, the original copies are owned by individual families.

Examples of events that the Rev Bridges included in the Almanac were: *"on 24th March 1895, the worst gale in living memory occurred, resulting in much damage to houses in the village and the loss of three thousand large trees on the Estate."*

"On November 13th 1906, the neighbourhood was much amused by the sudden incursion of German Gypsies, who encamped on Barton Hill, hurriedly locking up all pigs, cows, horses and fowls and barricading our homes, we hastened to witness this unwanted sight. Truly they were a motley crew of men, women and children, to the number of about ninety, under escort of a strong detachment of police. The whole carvanesy, including the horses would have been dear at a five pound note. The ladies as usual attracted my attention, their study of the English language appeared to have been principally confined to swear words, in which they showed an extraordinary efficiency. Their King who was attired in the simple garb of a country gentleman, is said to be bulging with bullion, but I saw no sign of that pomp and parade which are the usual accompaniments of Kings and courts. On the whole, we were not ill pleased when the royal procession slowly wended it's way down the village street and passed on to shed it's glamour elsewhere."

" Otters were frequently observed swimming in the river Ise. And in April 1907 , a young otter was found near the road bridge, that had been cut off from it's mother by rising floods. It was eventually rescued and taken to Lord Lilford's at Lilford who was a lover of wild life and he would ensure it a safe and happy future."

Agnes Picheley *"gave to the church of Warkton an aulter cloth and a sheete"* in 1530.

Until 1549 all church services were conducted in Latin, which is the same year that the first known Warkton church register appears. From 1548, all parishes were required to maintain records of christenings, marriages, and deaths, of everyone in the village. This was the year of the end of Henry VIIIs reign, and the order was confirmed by the boy King Edward VI.

There were few literate men in the county in those days who were able to write up the records. The parish chest would hold the records on "bits of paper or parchment". Later they were transferred into a leather bound book, probably by the parish clerk, although by law all events should have been entered in the book the day that they were performed. The same hand writing could be traced for many years and in Warkton's case they seem to have been written into the official book at the end of each year. In 1665, and again in 1716 there were no entries. The pages were left blank to be filled in later but this was never done.

Until 1754, christenings marriages and deaths were all recorded in one book, the first notice of banns of marriage was in 1699. After 1754 marriages were to be logged in a separate book with the signature of two witnesses added, this was to be called the New Style. The majority of those who were witnesses could not write so they signed with an X.

In 1812, an Act was passed that stated that christenings and burials were also to be recorded in separate books, but Warkton had been using independent books since 1763. The 1812 George Rose's Act also said that christenings must include the names, addresses and occupations of the parents, The burial entries were to state the age, address, and occupation of the deceased. But in Warkton an address could not be recorded until the 1890s when the houses were numbered.

The Burial in Wool Act of 1667 was intended to support the wool trade, and enacted that a corpse should be buried in wool only except any person who should die of the plague. A relative of the deceased had to sign an affidavit (recorded in the registers) that a burial in wool had taken place or else a fine of £5 was levied. In Warkton, there were 120 burials before the first mention of an affidavit was made in 1717. There were a small number who paid the £5 fine, these were mostly the Montagu family who were buried in lead coffins in the family vault. The above act was repealed in 1814 but had by then fallen into disuse.

In March 1810 the Enclosure Notice was read to the church congregation at Divine Service, and duly recorded in the church register. This notice derived it's legal authority from a private act of parliament of 1807 whereby the common lands of Warkton and Little Oakley were ordered for enclosure. The entry in the register is as coldly formal as one would expect it to be, but what must have been the feelings of the commoners of Warkton, when they heard that notice read. The old fields, the common and waste land were to be swept away. No longer would the cottager have pasture for his cow, nor a common to share with his neighbours. From hence forth he was landless, entirely dependant upon the wages which a master would pay him.

There are extant 38 wills/inventories of Warkton residents from the earliest Elinor Pitchley 1710 to Ann Cave 1857. Of these 16 concern yeoman farmers, 11 widows, 2 gardeners, 2 blacksmiths, 1 gamekeeper, 1 carpenter, 1 tanner, 1 labourer and 3 with no identified trade.

Febbruary ye 9d 17 20/21

I Mary Green of Warkton in the County of
Northampton being sick and Weak of Body, but
in perfect Strength of Mind and Memory recommend
my soul to God who gave it in hopes of a Resurrection to
Eternal Life through ye only Merits of Jesus Christ my
Redeemer, do make and ordain this my last will and
Testament in form and Manner following

Imprimis I will and Bequeath all my Land to my Son
John
Item I give to my Three Daughters Elizabeth Rebecca
and Hanah all my Goods Cattell Money & Clothes
whom I make joynt Executors of this my last
Will & Testament they paying my Lawful Debts
and Burying my Body in Christian Manner
Item to my Daughter Mary I give the Sum of Twenty shilling
Item to my Son John's Children, John Elizabeth
and Mary I will and bequeath ten shillings apie
in Witness Wherdof I have set my hand and Seal the
Day and year above written

Witnessed by us
Josias Pitckes
John Cobb
Ann Vandermeulen

Mary   Green
Her † Mark

A copy of Mary Greens Will of 1720

A copy of William Burditt's Inventory of 1733

A True and Perfect Inventory of the goods and Chattels of William Burditt late of Warkton in the county of Northampton deceesed taken and apprauyed the 3th Day of October 1733 by John green and Joseph Medas as follows

	£ s d
Item the purse and appareill	02:00:0
It in the best Chamber one bead and other lumber	03:00:0
In the other Chamber one bead and other lumber	01:10:0
In the Parler one bead and other lumber	01:00:0
In the hall one tabel and other lumber	00:10:0
Goods in the Kichin and in the Chamber ouer itt	01:00:00
the puter and brase	01 00 00
the Wheat	18:00:00
the barly	15:00:00
the Payes	10:00:00
one Wagan and one Cart	05:00:00
fiue horses	10:00:00
the gears and plows and other Metterlies	01:00:00
Six Cowrs and two Caloes	10:00:00
fifty sheep and lambs	12:10:00
the tillige and the dung	15:00:00
one hog and they hay and pulling	05:00:00
£	108:10 0

John Green
Joseph Meadows

Overseer's Vestry Meetings were held in the church usually quarterly. Any other meetings such as for village activities and affairs including political meetings were held in the village pub for a small charge until the new school opened in 1867 when they were admitted free.

The Overseer's Account 1818 records details such as:

Expenses at the visitation (to Wellingborough)	17s 0d
Paid for lock for church porch	1s 6d
Paid Thomas Meadows for church geats (gates)	7s 0d
Paid for cleaning church windows	7s 6d
Paid William Sharman for the clock	13s 6d
(an annual payment for winding the clock, ceased in 1926)	
Paid for washing the surples (surplices)	3s 0d
Paid for bottle of whin (wine)	5s 6d
Clarks wages	£1 5s 0d
Repairing church gates	£1 10s 6d
Repairing clock 3 times during the year	£1 2s 6d
Salary for teaching children half yearly	10s 0d
New bell ropes (this appears nearly every year)	£1 12s 6d
Repairing the church porch and whightwashing (whitewashing)	3s 6d
Carriage of stone and mortar for church wall	9s 0d
Paid Sam Charter for hatts for schoolchildren	8s 0d
Paid Mr Illif for repairing stow (stove)	7s 6d
Paid William Kirk for ale	9s 6d

The Overseer's Account 1840 records:
Two cwts coal 5s 4d this is the first mention of coal for use in the church, from then onwards it details 14 cwts to 1 ton per annum.

1844 at a Vestry Meeting on 9th April, Mr Melkin and Mr Panther were nominated as Churchwardens. Mr Ward and Mr Panther were nominated Overseers of the poor. Mr Ward and Mr Jones, were nominated surveyors of the roads. Every year there were nominations for the above, often different people. Most persons nominated did not stay many years in the job. There were exceptions with certain men staying in the position for long periods.

1848 candles for church 1s 0d. This is the first entry found for candles but after this date it is a regular entry. In the same year; paid Mr Wright for coffin cards and for mending a bell rope 4s 3d, mending school seats 3s 0d.

In1856: paid for a man with a cart and horse to Kettering for lead for the church 4s 0d, and a mat for the school 1s 6d.
1865: paid a man half a day for clearing snow from the roof 3s 0d.

1866: extra rates of £13 10s 0d were required towards defraying expenses attending the consecration of an additional portion of ground for the enlargement of the churchyard.

In October of this year, an Extraordinary General Meeting was called and it was unanimously resolved that it was desirable to close the old pathway leading from the gate near Mrs Russell's cottage,(number 12) and passing through the new portion of the churchyard. The Churchwardens were empowered to take the necessary legal steps to effect this.

At Vestry Meeting in 1913, Mr Ward the organist, applied for an increase in salary but funds were too low, and Mr Robert Brett proposed that a charge to view the monuments be set at 3d, and this proposal was carried.

In 1923, it was decided to insure the church contents for £8,000, and not to subscribe for the use of Kettering's fire engine but to support Kettering Hospital only. And in 1934, it was proposed that, *"to save mowing the churchyard to graze it with sheep."*

On March 31st 1851 there was a nationwide census as to how many people attended church services. At St Edmunds Church there were fifty in the general congregation and fifty seven Sunday School scholars. In the afternoon there were one hundred and twenty general congregation and again fifty seven scholars. The church has a seating capacity of two hundred and fifty persons.

In 1920, when the path to the west of the churchyard was in the course of being widened, a child's skeleton was discovered just below the surface, with no headstone or marker. It is assumed that this body was buried possibly at night at the time when most people could not afford a burial, or that it was illegitimate and the family did not want anyone to know of it. This child was decently re-interred.

Since the year 2000, an annual lecture has been given at St Edmunds for the edification of the local population. These have included such eminent speakers as the educationalist and author Gervase Phinn, Terry Waite and the writer and broadcaster Pam Rhodes. These lectures are sponsored by the John Warren Foundation. The foundation concentrates it's resources exclusively for the benefit of parishes in Northamptonshire, Lincolnshire and Nottinghamshire, (primarily on the repair, improvement and refurbishment of church buildings). It was first established in 1949, with it's earlier origins in a trust known as "Cannon Warren's Charitable Trust". It was founded by John Shrapnel Warren, rector of Willoughby Church, Lincoln in 1919.

St Edmunds Parish Charities

(taken form the Warkton Church register dated 1667)
"The Right Honourable Edward Lord Montagu be in present of our accounts. Willed

that it should be recorded in this our Town Book, that where as his late virtuous mother at her decease had bequeathed and the parish had received already, so as is before recorded anno-domini 1618 where upon the repayment of the said fifty shillings a year said Lord Montagu as bequeathed and confirmed to the Parish for ever the sum of six shillings and eight pence"

This payment was still being paid in 1835, no further records have been found.

The Hunt Charity

Edward Hunt by will dated 20th October 1674 bequeathed to Broughton, Kettering, Rothwell, Weekley and Warkton the rent from $2^1/4$ yardlands which he owned in Broughton, to be distributed to the poor or those most in need of the above parishes.

Warkton's share was 10s 0d to be paid on the 5th November. In 1707 it was 5s 0d and now called the "Noble Money". Throughout the nineteenth century it varied yearly from 6s 8d to £3 16s 0d. Once coal became readily available it was shared out in that commodity instead of money. In 1907 it was 13s 6d and the Rev Bridges said: *"it was such a trifling sum that he proposed the usual recipients toss up for it"*. In the 1930s it averaged £4 per annum with twelve recipients.

Warkton Church Charity

Formally known as the Warkton Poor's Lands. (referred to in the enclosure award of 1808) and that the original object of the charity was for the income to be used for the poor of Warkton. Over the years it became the custom for it to be used for the repairs to St Edmunds Church. In 1988 part of the church land off Deeble Road was gifted to the Church Commissioners for England for the siting of a new church building (now known as Christ The King)

In 1995 the Charity Commissioners approved a scheme amending the provision of the charity so that the primary use of income was to be applied towards the improvement, upkeep and repair of St Edmunds Church and the secondary use of income was to further the religious and other charitable work of the church in the ecclesiastical parish.

The Hickman Charity

Established under the will of Emma Hickman who died on January 30th 1954. It is admissible by the Rector and Churchwardens. The object of the charity is *"keeping in good and reverent order the Churchyard at Warkton"*.

The Panther Charity

Established on December 12th 1922. It is admissible by the Rector and Churchwardens. It is primarily *"for the maintenance and support of a Church of England Sunday School established in and for the Parish of Warkton, including the purchase of prizes for scholars attending such school"*.

St Edmunds Church 1872 taken from the north east corner, showing the first two graves in the new eastern 1870 churchyard extension, resulting in the church yard surrounding the church building.

Today there are two hundred and fifty nine grave stones still standing. Thirty seven of which are totally illegible. The earliest one is dated 17th April 1728 Mary Orpin wife of John.

The church C1890 taken from the north east corner of the churchyard

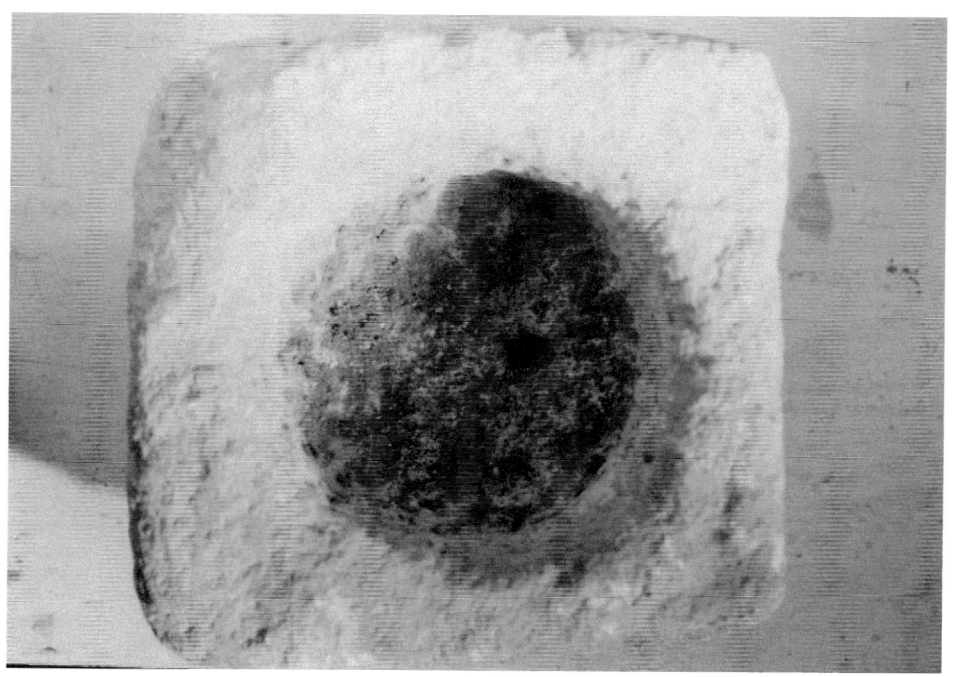

An ancient bowl that was found in the early 1700s in the churchyard.

The lepers window, on the south wall, where the afflicted persons would come to receive a blessing and communion.

Outside the West Door.

This picture was taken in 1882 at the request of the Rev Henry Stobart, so that he could remember his Warkton friends when he left the village.

Seated left to right they were:

Mary Cave she was the village dressmaker, she lived at number 14.

Sarah Issitt she lived at number 4

William Issitt Sarah's father and was horsekeeper at Panthers tannery.

Margaret Russell who lived at number 12, and ran the village laundry, collecting and delivering with a donkey and cart. She used a mangle that was seven feet long and filled with stones to give it weight.

William Issitt. He used two sticks because of a lifetime of rheumatism, and was nicknamed Tanner Will to distinguish him from two other William Issitts in the village. He worked at the tannery and lived all his life in the house that was in front of Isebrook Farm, which was demolished in 1904. As a treat he used to give villagers cows tails and jowls to take home to roast for a meal.

Ann Meadows, she lived at number 32.

Bet Goode, she was well known for the caps that she wore and for always smoking a clay pipe. She worked for Miss Melking of Elm Farm and was also a flax spinner, gathering sheep's wool and using a spinning wheel, well into her eighties.

Standing left to right:

Lucy Taylor who lived at number 17 she was the caretaker of the church and the village midwife.

Charlotte Mutton lived at number 40, she used to make ginger beer for Warkton Feast, on Whit Sunday.

Jane Issitt, the wife of William, (Tanner Will).

William Bamford. He was responsible for the upkeep of the village roads, and walked to Northampton Race Course to witness the last public hanging in Northamptonshire, a round trip of 32 miles.

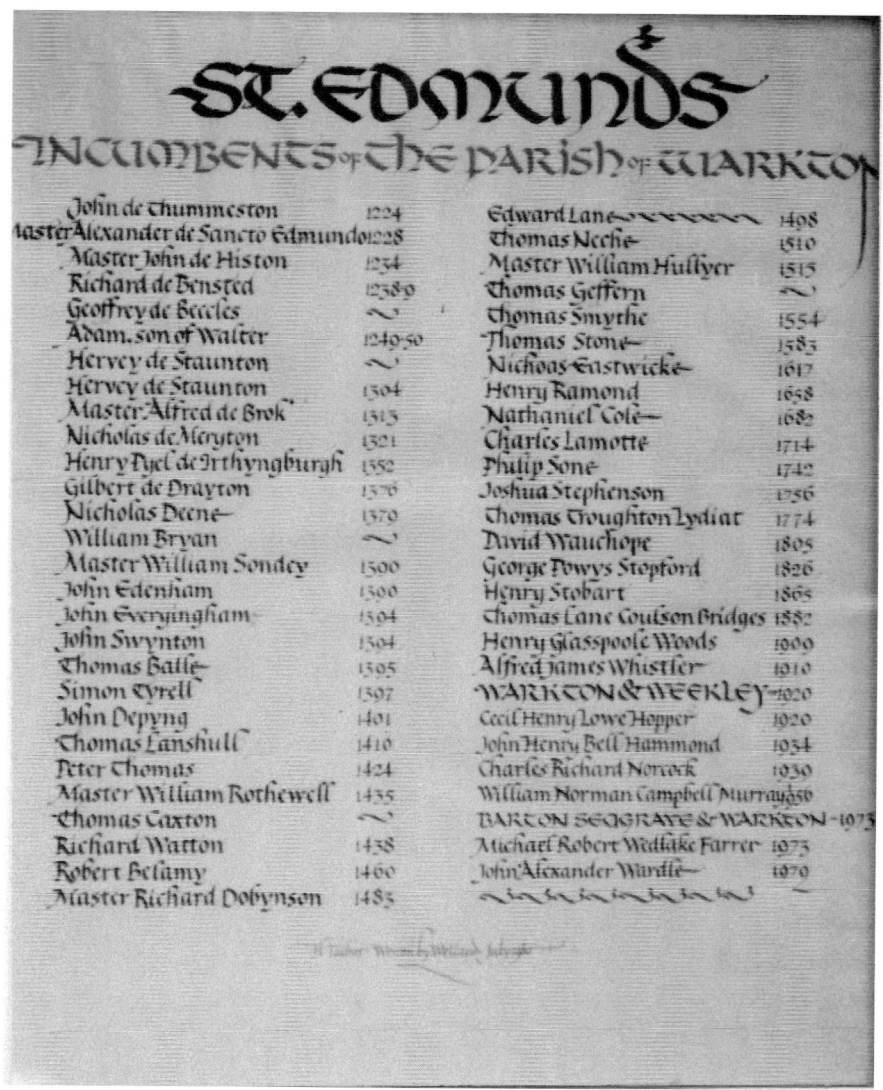

This plaque is on the vestry wall and lists the church incumbents from 1224 until 1979, there are fifty four names inscribed here.

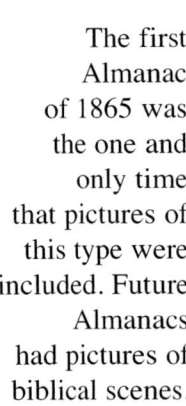

Henry Stobart
1865 - 1881

The Rev Henry Stobart the incumbent from 1865 to 1881.

In 1867 he started a yearly village Almanac, which gave a weekly prayer and Bible tract. Births, Marriages and Deaths were recorded together with specific items of news, and comments. This was distributed to everyone who attended church, and was approximately 2ft x 2ft 6, designed to be hung up on the wall.

The first Almanac of 1865 was the one and only time that pictures of this type were included. Future Almanacs had pictures of biblical scenes.

JANUARY XXXI DAYS.
THE WINTER FOLD.

FEBRUARY XXVIII DAYS.
SKATING ON THE SERPENTINE.

MARCH XXXI DAYS.
CLEARING THE WOODS.

APRIL XXX DAYS.
THE SWALLOWS NEST.

MAY XXXI DAYS.
GATHERING THE MAY.

JUNE XXX DAYS.
DRINKING FOUNTAIN.

JULY XXXI DAYS.
HAY HARVEST.

AUGUST XXXI DAYS.
WHEAT HARVEST.

SEPTEMBER XXX DAYS.
COVENT GARDEN MARKET.

OCTOBER XXXI DAYS.
THE FRUIT HARVEST.

NOVEMBER XXX DAYS.
THE WINTER TORRENT.

DECEMBER XXXI DAYS.
NEW CATTLE MARKET, LONDON.

W·ARKTON PARISH CHURCH.

THE following few directions and recommendations are made to the Parishioners in view of the Re-opening of their Parish Church :—

The Church will henceforth have *no Seats appropriated either to families or individuals*, and the Churchwardens look to the Parishioners to seat themselves, as they enter Church, in a quiet and orderly manner, every one seeking by courtesy and kindness to be accommodating to his neighbour. If Selfishness and Pride be left without, and only Love and Humility be brought within the Church, the Wardens feel sure that the leaving the body of the Church *free to all*, will be proved, by experience, to be the most convenient arrangement, as it certainly is the one which is most founded on law and justice, and in closest agreement with the letter and spirit of God's Word.

It is requested that *no private cushions or hassocks be brought into the Church*, except for anyone who, through age or infirmity, may not be able to kneel like others, and requires a higher hassock. The whole of the sittings will be amply provided with the same good-sized kneeling mats, which can also be used as cushions to sit upon, should any one think this is required.

The kneeling mats should *never be used for putting the feet upon*, and should be *hung up at the close of the Service* on the hooks provided for the purpose. *Particular attention is requested to these two points.*

There is an arrangement for holding hats under the seat of every alternate person, and it is recommended that the hats should be put under the seat *in front*, as less likely to be in the way when kneeling.

As persons will constantly be sitting in different seats, it will be better that no Bibles, Prayer books, or Hymn books be left in the Church. Any books forgotten to be taken out of the Church will be put together on the sill of the window next to the Font.

It is hoped that the front seat next to the Pulpit, on the north side of the nave, will be kindly allowed to be always left for the use of the most aged of the parish.

The Churchwardens wish that *the seats in the north aisle* be chiefly occupied by men ; the seats in *the south aisle* by women ; and those *under where the old gallery used to be* by the school-children.

On the morning of the Re-opening, the Choir and Churchwardens will meet the Bishop and Rector at the entrance of the Churchyard, on the Rectory side, at five minutes before eleven, and the Parishioners are requested to follow them in an orderly manner through the Churchyard into the Church, by the western (the Tower) door. *The Church will not be opened beforehand.* Psalms 84 and 122 will be chanted as the procession passes into the Church.

A Collection on the day of Re-opening will be made for the purchase of a new pulpit, the expenses of the alterations having so increased that it has been impossible to provide one. It is hoped that the Parishioners and their friends will liberally contribute towards this, and that the want will be supplied by the coming Easter. The cost of it will be about £50.

The Rector takes this occasion to request, that whenever the Holy Communion is celebrated, the non-communicants will not leave until after the Prayer for the Church Militant, in order that *all* may have *the opportunity of giving their alms.*

HENRY STOBART, Rector.

JOHN LANCUM, } Churchwardens.
THOS. DAWSON, }

A copy of the new rules for the parishioners, implemented by the Rev Stobart in 1868.

The Rev Stobart
and his wife
together with
their nine
daughters
C1870.
The Stobart
family worked
tirelessly for
the good of the
village, starting
an evening
reading facility

in the school, and later developing this into an evening club and participating in
village celebrations and entertainments. Their daughters were well known for their
musical talents which were much admired at social events.

Thomas Lane Coulson Bridges
1882 - 1909

The Rev Thomas Lane
Coulson Bridges incumbent
from 1882 to 1909
He continued the village work
that the Stobart family had
commenced including the
Almanac, that ceased when he
left Warkton. He took a great
interest in the school and was a
strict disciplinarian. When any
child misbehaved at school they
were sent to him for a suitable
punishment, this was usually
a caning.

The Rev Alfred James Whistler incumbent from 1910-1920 He had been a former Royal Naval Chaplain. In 1885 he was awarded the Egypt Medal and the Khedive's Bronze Star. The ships that he served on included, Hercules 1880-1887, Euphrates 1887-1890 and The Aurora in 1890. His incumbency included looking after St Mary's Church Weekley during a five year interregnum, and he was held in great esteem and affection by the parishioners. His children played a full part in the village and distinguished themselves during the First World War. He expected regular attendance at church and would visit those who defaulted.

The Rev Cecil Henry Lowe Hopper incumbent from 1920 to 1935. This picture shows his wife and their car in 1932.
In 1921, despite much local opposition, both at Weekley and Warkton, St Edmunds

Warkton was joined with St Marys Weekley as a united benefice.
The Rev Hopper continued to live at The Vicarage Weekley and supported both village's activities and events.

St Edmunds taken from the north side, showing the old clock which failed in 1955. This clock having been silent for ten years, was eventually replaced in 1965 following a generous donation from Major Henry Knight.

Mrs. Chas. Wells Passes Away

Mrs Charles Wells a farmer at Elm Tree Farm in Warkton, who lived through six reigns. She was born in Warkton in August 1817, her parents being Mr and Mrs John Melkin. When three years old she was led to the playground at Warkton to see the decorations displayed to celebrate the coronation of George IV. When a young girl she attended a school at Kettering, managed by the Rev Abner Brown, then a school in Market Harborough.

Her father was a member of Lord Cardigan's Cavalry, he wore a very smart uniform, which was green and gold with a triangular plumed hat. Mrs Wells remembered the opening of the first railway and was married to Charles Wells in 1842. She made a visit with her husband to the Great Exhibition in Hyde Park London in 1851. She saw Queen Victoria when she passed through Kettering on her way to Burghley House, her husband acting as one of the Guards of Honour at the entrance to the White Hart Hotel (Royal Hotel Kettering) where Her Majesty stayed. Another of her characteristics was her interest in architectural matters. Her home at Warkton being striking proof of the remarkable gift she had for designing highly effective structural alterations. Her beautiful garden testified to the interest that she took in the beauties of nature. Generous to a degree and a lover of the church, Mrs Wells donated many beautiful gifts, including an organ in 1877, and two new bells to commemorate Queen Victoria's Jubilee in 1888. The organ was built by Messrs Walker and Sons of London, and has three hundred and ten pipes. It was originally fitted on the south side of the chancel and was hand pumped by one of the choir boys. The organ was used for the first time on St Paul's day January 25th 1877. In this position it took up a lot of the light coming in from the east window and almost hid one of the monuments. Consequently, almost one hundred years later, in the 1970s the organ was removed and placed where the original musician's gallery had been, resulting in a new gallery being constructed.

At this time the magnificent choir stalls were removed from the chancel, these had also been donated by Mrs Wells in 1901 in memory of Thomas Jones who was killed in a harvest field in 1898. Mrs Wells donated the first set of surplices for the choir in 1901.

In 1904 new hassocks were also donated by Mrs Wells, who died in 1910 aged 93 at Orton, where she had moved to in 1904, to be looked after by her relatives in the last years of her life.

The Chancel taken before the alterations.
This photograph shows the organ which was donated by Mrs Wells in 1877, situated adjacent to the monuments on the south chancel wall, and the wrought iron gates. In the 1970s this organ was dismantled and rebuilt in the new tower gallery where it has remained ever since. The choir stalls were also removed in order to facilitate the enhancement of the visual impact of the four monuments. Prior to this organ donation in 1877, the previous tower gallery was used for the musicians and the choir during church services. Charles Routham who died in 1940 related that his father played a bass-viol there, and he could remember when a string band was displaced by a barrel organ that could play a limited number of hymn tunes.

The Tower Gallery 2006.

The East window behind the war memorial taken in 1920 at the time that the memorial was being dedicated.

1920, the dedication of the War Memorial, taken from the church roof. This was an occasion when the whole village attended the ceremony.

Flight Lieutenant Harold Whistler DSO. DFC unveiling the War Memorial in 1920.

The Evening Telegraph article reporting the occasion referred to some three to four hundred people attending the unveiling and dedication on Passion Sunday afternoon.

The Cross was made of Clipsham stone, by Messrs Morris and Sons of Kettering. Harold Whistler said *"I unveil this Cross to the Glory of God and to the glorious memory of the men from this parish who gave their lives in The Great War"*. He then read the names and particulars of each of those from the village who lost their lives.

HONOURED DEAD.

Memorial Cross Unveiled at Warkton

In the presence of three or four hundred people a Memorial Cross, erected in Warkton Churchyard in honour of the men from the village who gave their lives for King and Country in the Great War, was unveiled and dedicated on Passion Sunday afternoon.

The memorial stands due east from the altar, and takes the form of a Cross. Surmounting two octagonal bases is a square die stone and cap (the former having four panels containing the incriptions in raised letters) and octagonal shaft, with trefoil Cross, the total height being eleven feet. At the foot a path is bordered by a kerb. It is made of Clipsham stone by Messrs. Morris and Sons, Kettering.

The inscriptions on the four panels are as follow :—

"To the glorious memory of the men from this parish who gave their lives in the Great War, 1914—1919."

"Archibald Charles Sargeant, October 11th, 1917; Arthur Fred Bagshaw, October 15th, 1917; Horace Mutton, December 15th, 1917; Eric Geo. Bagshaw, April 13th, 1918; William Henry Brett Wales, August 21st, 1918. 'Their name liveth for evermore.'"

"Greater love hath no man than this that a man lay down his life for his friends."

"Erected by relatives, parishioners, and friends as a token of honour and respect."

A bottle had been placed in a cavity in the stone die before the cap was affixed thereon Inside the bottle, which was put there by Miss Wales, is a parchment bearing the names and records of the Warkton men who made the great sacrifice, and the names of the Rector, the churchwardens, and committee. The latter comprised: The Rev. A. J. Whistler (Rector), Messrs. T. A. Turner, T. J. Sargeant, Ar. Rippin, Ernest Mutton, and Horace Patrick; churchwardens, Messrs. T. A. Turner, and R H. Brett.

THE SERVICE.

In the early part of the afternoon the sounds of a muffled peal emanating from the Warkton tower were heard over a wide area. Many people were wending their way to the village—a large number coming from Kettering on a glorious afternoon. Near the school the Union Jack was at half-mast.

The Memorial Cross unveiled at Warkton in 1920.

The South porch. In February 1915, a lady from Kettering, who was suffering from depression, came to the village and here in the porch her baby son was found dead, she was beside him, unconscious. She was taken to Kettering Hospital, and, after recovering from her injuries, sadly she was charged with infanticide for which she served a two year sentence. After this tragedy the porch was closed until it was rededicated by The Bishop of Peterborough six weeks later.

St Edmunds Church Choir 1928. In 1875 there were twenty two men in the choir but in 1900 the Rev Bridges complained that on a number of Sundays no men were in the choir.

Under the Rev Hopper, the choir flourished, due to the fact that boys of school age were encouraged to join the choir, sing at school and at church services and festivals. Sixty six percent of the choir at this time were male.

Church Choir 1952

The choir at this period comprised fifty percent male members.

During the 1990s the choir were winners at the Oundle festival for 3 successive years in the village choir section.

Extending the church heating system 1930
Whilst excavating to install under floor
heating pipes, a coffin was unearthed
facing south, containing a young female
with evidence of her hair still in perfect
condition, the coffin was resealed and left
in position. Her preservation was due to
the below floor atmospheric conditions,
and was remarkable as this coffin had
been buried for approximately 400 years.
With the electric heating in use today the
old heating system was made redundant. In
the 1950s the underfloor boiler and pipe
system was decommissioned completely
and is no longer visible.

School children sorting the excavated rubble from the church in 1930.
The rubble was found to contain a vast array of human bones. In order to treat
these human remains with due dignity, the school children were organised to
separate all these bones from the rubble so that they could be decently re-interred
in the church yard near the south wall. In 1990 a new roof draining system was
being installed, and in front of the vestry door a large pile of human bones was
unearthed. These were also decently re-interred near the south wall.

Repairing the church roof in 1936. These repairs were necessary due to the discovery of deathwatch beetle. During the work on the roof a large void was discovered above the south aisle, which resulted in far more repair work than had previously been anticipated.

The restoration of the tower that was undertaken in February 1965.

In 1936 the Duke and Duchess of Kent spent their honeymoon at Boughton House. In anticipation of their attendance at church on Sunday morning, large crowds gathered outside the church. Unfortunately the crowds were disappointed as the honeymooners did not appear. Similar scenes were seen at Weekley the following Sunday.

THE DISAPPOINTED CROWD of visitors who assembled outside Warkton Church on Sunday morning in

1993 Retuning of the church bells.
In 1700 St Edmunds had four church bells, one fell down the tower and was broken in the early 1800s.
The Tenor bell was made in 1638 by Hugh Watts of Leicester. The two remaining bells were cast by Thomas Eayre of Bellfoundry Lane Kettering, one in 1781 the other in 1761 the year in which Thomas Eayre's business closed down.

In 1888 two more bells were donated by Mrs Wells. These were cast by J Taylor and company of Loughborough.

The five bells were removed in 1993, retuned at the Whitechapel Bellfoundry in London, and returned to the church ready for their rehanging. At the same time a new sixth bell was donated to the church by Major Henry Knight, whose family had enjoyed close connections with the village for over one hundred years. He donated the bell, cast at Whitechapel, "to the honour of men and women of Northamptonshire who served in the Royal Signals during the Second World War and subsequent conflicts."

The Princess Royal visiting
St Edmunds Church June 1938
The Princess Royal was a regular
visitor to Boughton House. During
these visits she attended services at
either Warkton or Weekley church.
She is seen here leaving the church
on the right of the Rev Hammond.
The Duchess drove the car with The
Princess Royal back to Boughton
House and the gentlemen walked to
the house by the private path.

After worshipping, with other members of the house party, at Warkton Church on Sunday morning, the Princess Royal left accompanied
by the Rector (the Rev. J. H. B. Hamond, M.A.). Later, on the suggestion of the Duke of Buccleuch, the famous monuments in the chancel
were inspected.

For several minutes after church on Sunday the Princess Royal, the
Earl of Harewood and the Duke of Buccleuch enjoyed an interesting
chat with Mr. J. A. Gotch, J.P., of Weekley Rise, before taking their
leave. The Princess expressed to Mr. Gotch her pleasure at having
attended the beautiful church, with which she had been much impressed, and discussed with him the possibility of the removal of the
organ from the chancel, so that the monuments could be displayed better.

The Princess Royal outside St Edmunds church in June 1938 she was a guest at
Boughton House.

AT WARKTON CHURCH.

Princess Inspects Celebrated Statuary.

On Sunday morning the Princess Royal, the Earl of Harewood, the Duke and Duchess of Buccleuch, their younger daughter (Lady Caroline Scott), and other members of the house party, attended divine service at Warkton Church.

Long before the bells of the church had begun to peal, people from the district flocked to the village, and a squad of police under Supt. A. J. Norris and Inspector A. J. Chapman, directed the traffic.

At a few minutes to eleven the Royal party arrived. Three cars conveyed them, the Duke of Buccleuch driving the first. The Princess Royal, in a speckled grey coat, with brown hat and fur, and carrying a brown handbag with a gold clasp, was in the second, with the Earl of Harewood and other visitors.

At the church door they were met by the Rector (the Rev. J. H. B. Hamond, M.A.), and the churchwardens (Mr. C. E. Lamb, and Mr. G. O. West), and were conducted to the two front pews on either side of the centre aisle.

The Princess Royal, the Earl of Harewood, and the Duke and Duchess of Buccleuch occupied the pew on the right, and from here the visitors could see the celebrated Buccleuch memorial statuary.

AN ADDED MEANING.

Devoutly the Princess followed the service as it was intoned by the Rector, and during the reading of the lessons, from Isaiah VI and St. Mark I, sat back and listened carefully as the verses were spoken by Mr. Hamond.

The hymns, "Holy, Holy, Holy, Lord God Almighty," "Three in One and One in Three" and "Bright the Vision" were sung, and the prayer "for Queen Elizabeth, Mary, the Queen Mother, Princess Elizabeth and all the Royal family" seemed to the congregation in that beautiful little church to take on an added meaning and reverence.

As the mixed choir chanted Psalms 29 and 33, the Princess Royal also joined in reverently.

This is how the visit by the Princess Royal was reported in 1938.

After the singing of the second hymn, Mr. Hamond delivered a short sermon from the text Isaiah VI. 3. "One cried unto another and said 'Holy, Holy, Holy is the Lord of Hosts. The whole earth is full of His glory.'"

Mr. Hamond spoke quietly and simply of the change in Isaiah's life. Then he told how Columbus, when he set out to discover the new world, saw three peaks on the horizon. Upon sailing nearer, he found them to be one island, which he named Trinidad, and which was Spanish for Trinity.

"You and I," he said, "as we sail over the sea of life, are going towards a country which, at present we know not, and there rise before us three peaks by which we steer our course, God the Father, God the Son and God the Holy Spirit."

At the conclusion of the service, the Princess knelt in prayer for a few moments and then left the church with her host and hostess and their friends.

As they did so, the congregation of parishioners stood, and the organist, Mr. A. P. J. Ward, played "Pastorale" by Varley Roberts and an Impromptu.

They walked to the gate, and then, on the suggestion of the Duke, the Princess Royal and her husband returned to the church to see the statuary.

As they left the church again, Mr. J. A. Gotch, J.P., of Weekley Rise, who had been in the congregation, was introduced to the Princess Royal and the Earl of Harewood, and the Royal visitors conversed animatedly with him.

Only two cars were used for the return journey to Boughton House, the first of which was driven by the Duchess of Buccleuch. The Duke, the Earl of Harewood and other male members of the party returned by the private footpath.

All members of the house party attended the service except Lord George Scott, the Earl of Pembroke, the Right Hon. Winston Churchill and Mrs. Churchill.

DUCHESS OF KENT AT WARKTON

The Duchess of Kent leaving Warkton Church in 1948, a guest of the Duke and Duchess of Buccleuch.

ESCORTED by the rector of Weekley and Warkton (the Rev. C. R. Norcock), the Duchess of Kent and her host and hostess from Boughton House, the Duke and Duchess of Buccleuch, leave Warkton Parish Church after attending morning service on Sunday.

The Duchess of Kent was a gracious figure in an all-black ensemble. She wore a lightweight dust coat with loose three-quarter sleeves over a dress, and a striking straw picture hat with an upturned velvet brim.

Her jewellery was a brooch placed high on the left shoulder of her coat, a silver and gold charm bracelet on her left wrist, a treble pearl necklace with a large pearl and diamond clasp, and pearl and diamond drop earrings.

The Duchess of Buccleuch wore a black two-piece with a pleated skirt, pearl necklace and small black hat.

There were a good number of disappointed film fans among the large crowd that gathered outside the church. Douglas Fairbanks, who was among the guests at Boughton for the week-end, did not attend the service.

St Edmunds Church taken in 2006. showing the new extensions built either side of the tower, to the west end of the church in 1997. The north extension houses a church office and a small cloakroom. The Warren Room on the south side

includes the magnificent stained glass window, of 1877, that was re-sited at the time of the alterations, to be on an exterior facing wall. This room is used by the thriving Sunday School as well as social church gatherings and meetings. The Warren Foundation charity is pleased to have supported St Edmunds Church at various times over the years and latterly with the furnishing of the Warren Room.

The School

The earliest record of a school is in the year 1619, when the Rev Nicholas Latham, Parson of Barnwell St Andrew, Northamptonshire, endowed the school in the village of Weekley for the children of Warkton and Weekley. He constituted Sir Edward 1st Lord Montagu and his heirs to be closely involved with the school. In 1770, Sir Edward Montagu's descendant, Lord John Montagu, Marquess of Monthermer, died at the age of 35 and his sister Elizabeth inherited the Boughton Estate. She had previously married Henry the 3rd Duke of Buccleuch, consequently, the Montagu name ceased and the Buccleuch family name was adopted as it is still to this day. The Buccleuch family has been closely associated with Warkton School throughout its life, and visited regularly as well as giving financial assistance in the form of equipment and improved facilities from time to time as an evident need was identified.

Weekley endowed school 1624.

This is the inscription over the doorway of the schoolhouse in Weekley which was built after the founder Nicholas Latham's death. It will be noted that the inscription referred to children, which indicates that Latham was concerned about the education of girls as well as boys.

The salary of the master of this school was £8 per annum, and £3 for maintenance. The schoolhouse still survives in the village. It is a single storey building of local limestone. A small wing was added in the 19th century when it was still in use as a school. It was eventually closed in 1936 and was used as the Boughton Estate office. It is now a private house.

We know that from 1619 children from Warkton attended the free school at Weekley. Up until the nineteenth century, until the new school opened in 1867, children up to the age of eight years old could attend school in the cottage that is now number 43. Here the children were taught basic reading, writing and arithmetic. If after eight years of age a child wanted further schooling, they had to go to Weekley, walking over the fields to the school and they paid one penny per week for the privilege. In the 1836 Overseer's account there appears for the first time a payment of one guinea to Mr Gilbert for teaching children. This fee was paid on a half yearly basis for a number of years.

In 1848 a teacher by the name of Charlotte Ingram, aged twenty five, came from Trowbridge in Wiltshire to be school mistress, and in 1851 was assisted by Lucy Potter aged nineteen of Warkton. In Whelans Directory of 1849, it notes that for

"Werkton there is an infant school free to all children under eight years of age, supported by the Duchess of Buccleuch"

In this year there were four boys and thirteen girls under the age of eight, who were taught there, Miss Ingram was still there in 1861.

It became evident that there would be a need for a new school within the village of Warkton because of the imminent School Act, which was designed to require all children to attend school regularly. Thus in 1867, at the expense of the 5th Duke of Buccleuch a school was built to accommodate up to eighty children from Warkton.

In the late 1860s Miss Isabella Fryer aged twenty eight from Monmouth in Wales, came to take over at the new school. In 1880 a further act made it compulsory for all children up to the age of ten to attend school. This age limit was raised in 1893 to eleven and in 1899 to twelve.

In 1891 there were eleven boys and twenty one girls on the register. Miss Ada Fairchild, aged 30 from London was the school mistress, living at number 43, the school house.

The school was proving to be a success by 1879, in November of this year it was inspected by Mr Simpson, the government inspector. The teacher Miss Brooks had 21 pupils to be examined. All of these passed in reading skills and 19 passed in writing and spelling skills. The inspector reported *"the school is very successfully conducted"*.

In 1881 the Diocesan Inspector in religious knowledge reported that *"the elder children showed a good knowledge of Prayer-book and Catholism, cultural success was also evident, and that the school was satisfactory."*

At the beginning of the 20th century the link between the school and the church was still very strong.

On 7th March 1900 the Diocesan Bishop, Bishop Carr-Glyn came to visit Warkton and spent some time in the school. The sixth Duke of Buccleuch took a keen interest in the school and in September he provided it with a new teacher's writing table and new desks. Following this addition of new equipment the School Inspector, Mr Cartwright inspected the school and reported favourably, resulting in a good government grant subsequently being received.

In September 1903, Balfour's Education Act was passed. This empowered Local Authorities to provide elementary and secondary education, thereby superseding the old School Boards. This meant that His Grace was no longer liable to supply Warkton school with any of it's requirements, these would hence forth would be provided by the Local Education Committee.

This building was used until 1961 when the school eventually closed. From this date it has been in use as the Village Hall for the resident community.

A notice giving details of the New Elementary Education Act

"IMPORTANT TO PARENTS AND EMPLOYERS OF CHILDREN

The following is a correct statement of the law is parishes where there are no Bye-laws.

Where Bye-law have been made, either by a School Board or School Attendance Committee, the clauses in the first paragraph numbered (1) and (2) will be varied according to the Bye-laws.

These clauses are a correct statement of the law as regards employers (in all parishes) who are not subject to attend the schools provided for them.

THE NEW ELEMENTARY EDUCATION ACT declares that it is the duty of all parents to cause their children to attend the Schools provided for them.

In order to prevent the neglect of such parental duty, it declares that:-

(1) No child may go to work under 10 years of age.

(2) Children over 10 years of age may go to work only if they have first obtained a Certificate, stating either that they have passed the Third Standard at School or that they have attended a certified efficient School 250 times during each year for three previous years.

Every Employer of a children not having one of these Certificates is liable to a penalty of £2.

Parents employing their children in any trade, or for the purposes of gain, are considered "Employers" and are liable to the same penalty.

This penalty will not be enforced if the Employer can show —

(1) That there is no efficient School within two miles of the child's residence.

(2) That the child is only employed during holidays or out of school hours.

(3) That the child is employed with the permission of the Local Authority during such times as the hay and harvest and hop-picking seasons.

If any child above the age of five years, and who has no excuses on account of sickness or on account of there being no School within two miles, is found habitually wandering in idleness, or in the company of bad children, the Parent of such child, after due warning, may be fined 5s. And if the Parent still neglects his duty, the fine can be repeated again and again at intervals of two weeks, and finally, if the Parent, if judged able, will have to contribute to its support.

In certain cases when a child has been very regular in attendance at school for two or more years, and has before the age of 11, passed the Fourth Standard at the School Examination, the Act provides that, as a Reward, its future School-fees, for a period not exceeding three years, shall be paid by the Government.

The penalty for forgoing a Certificate, or for false representation as to age, is £2.

A photograph taken in 1975, of number 43, The School House – as it was called in the nineteenth century. In 1906 this house caught fire and suffered considerable damage, caused by a beam that ran across the main room into the chimney breast and ignited when the chimney caught fire. This unfortunately happened quite frequently where the main house beam end rested on the chimney breast.

Admission Number.	Date of Admission on the Roll.	Name of Child. (Christian and Surname.)	Birthday. (Exact date.)	Name and Address of Parent or Guardian.
	18 76	Names of Children now on register 1876		
1	1869	William Clifford	Jan 25 '66	John Clifford Warkton
2	1869	John Robinson	Aug 5 '64	Joseph Robinson Warkton
3	1869	John Toseland	Dec 2 '66	Matthew Toseland Warkt.
4	1870	Thomas Fletcher	May 1 '67	John Fletcher
5	1872	Arthur Lawrence	Jan 11 '68	Jno. R. Lawrence
6	1872	George Fletcher	May 1 '70	John Fletcher
7	1872	John Clifford	Jan 5 '68	John Clifford
8	1873	George Robinson	Jan 19 '70	Joseph Robinson
9	1873	George Bagshawe	June 8 '70	George Bagshawe
10	1873	Ashton Goodman	July 7 '70	Sarah Ann Goodman
4	1872	Walter Smith	April 7 '69	Isaac Smith
12	1874	Edwin Clifford	Feb 3 '72	John Clifford
13	1875	Albert Mutton	Dec 15 '72	Joseph Mutton
14	1876	William Fletcher	Oct 4 '72	John Fletcher
15	1869	Catherine Harris	Jan 8 '66	William Harris
16	1868	Elizabeth Lawrence	Aug 30 '65	Jno Lawrence
17	1869	Fanny Mutton	May 18 '66	Joseph Mutton
18	1870	Ellen Chaplin	Aug 7 '67	George Chaplin
19	1871	Ellen Goodman	Jan 25 '68	Sarah R. Goodman
20	1871	Ellen Robinson	Feb 3 '68	Joseph Robinson
21	1870	Mary Jane Bagshawe	Nov 20 '67	George Bagshawe
22	1873	Harriet Lawrence	April 20 '70	Jno Lawrence
23	1873	Edith Harris	July 6 '70	William Lawrence Nov
24	1871	Laura Harris	May 12 '68	William Harris
25	1869	Elizabeth Smith	Dec 22 '66	Isaac Smith
26	1872	Elizabeth Taylor	July 31 '69	William Taylor
27	1871	Emily Mutton	Oct 11 '68	Joseph Mutton
28	1872	Rosina Bagshawe	Jan 11 '69	George Bagshawe
29	1868	Anne Fletcher	March 1 '65	John Fletcher
30	1875	Delpha Robinson	Oct 13 '71	Joseph Robinson
31	1875	Sarah Mutton	July 25 '71	Joseph Mutton
32	1875	Kate Smith	Dec 28 '71	Isaac Smith
33	1875	Fanny Bagshawe	June 28 '72	George Bagshawe
..				

A copy of the school register from 1869 showing the first admissions to the
new school.

This is the earliest school photograph of the Warkton pupils in 1902, taken outside the school building, the boy in the centre is holding a slate, all pupils used slates to write on.

1909.

May 10. Miss S. Loveday, Assistant Teacher
at Burton Latimer C.E. Inft.
School commenced here as
temporary teacher of the
Infant class.

" 10. S.A. O.Mc Palmer visited this morning.

" 10. I have allowed the elder boys
the use of a corner piece
of the playground for a garden
in which they have set a
variety of seeds for the

Register   observation of their growth.
May 14   examined register - Correct -
                    Thomas A Turner

" 14 Weekly attendance percentage
reached 94.8.

" 17 Miss Annie Sharp, (Uncert)
Assistant Teacher at Flore
C.E. Schools, commenced
temporary duty with the
Infant Class. Miss Loveday

Thomas Arthur Turner the village constable wrote his report after a school visit
on February 22nd 1909. It was one of his duties to inspect the school register on a
monthly basis. Being a church school the Rector was obliged to attend at least
once a week.

[National Society's Form No. 108.

DIOCESE of _Peterborough_

RURAL DEANERY of _Weston_

No. 94

REPORT OF RELIGIOUS INSTRUCTION.

Warkton SCHOOL.

Mixed & Infant DEPARTMENT.

Inspected _27th June_ 1910

Present 30. On Books 39. Correspondent.

It gives the Inspector much pleasu
to visit this School again & to find that
Religious Instruction has been so well impa
by Miss Lawrence & Miss Cawston.

The Standard children presented a qui
satisfactory syllabus and answered very w
on all parts of it.

The Infant Group showed a wonderf
knowledge of a liberal number of Bible Sto
Even the youngest infants were able to ans
with intelligence and without shyness.
This Group deserves a new set of Bible
Pictures.

W. W. Dennett

A school inspection report dated June 1910

116

Empire day was commemorated every year until 1950s with the Duke of
Buccleuch being in attendance most years. On 24th May 1911 the following
entry is recorded in the school log book.

May

May 1st May Day holiday given (whole day)

" 2nd S.A.O. visited this morning.

" 5th Several children have been absent
this week through illness.
Aver: Attendance 28.1
Percentage   90.7.

" 8th Two infants admitted today
One left.
32 now on Books.

" 12th Percentage of Attendance 95.3.
Average   30.5

17th Examined the registers & found them
correct; 31 present

" 19th George Turner granted a
total exemption certificate.
Average attendance 30.8
Percentage 96.2.

" 24th Being Empire Day lessons have
back given on Patriotism
the attainment of the Colonies etc
Organised games have
also been indulged in

June 16th | Coronation Holiday (One Week)

June 26 | Re. opened school today.
Admitted two infants! Thomas
Banham & Sydney Mutton.
On Books = 33
No: present this morning = 32.

During the Coronation holiday the
N.C.C. sent a large flag. A
permanent staff has also
been erected in the playground.
The flag will be hoisted at
Festivals etc.

June 28 | Terminal Examination
started today.

June 30 | Percentage for Week = 96·3.
Average " " = 31·8

June 29. | Visit of Mr Elliot this
morning.

School log book entry of 26th June 1911 records the flag pole being installed in the school playground.

In the Millennium year 2000 the Parish Council arranged for the purchase of a new Union flag, a St George's flag and a flag pole. These are flown at appropriate dates throughout the year and are much appreciated by current village residents.

Hoisting the Union flag on Empire Day 1931.

9.15 – 9.20	Registers closed
9.20 – 9.30	Hoisting of Flag. National Anthem.
9.30 – 9.45	Singing — Patriotic Song "My own country"
9.45 – 10.15	Empire Day Lesson ? Geography of the Empire our duties as its citizens
10.15 – 10.45	Arithmetic
10.45 – 11 o'clock	Recreation
11 – 11.30	Spelling — Gt Britain's imports from various parts of the Empire
11.30 – 12	Pencil Drawing & Pastel Work — Empire Flags.
	" " " " continued
1.30 – 2	" " "
2 – 2.30	Organised Game — Cricket.
2.30 – 2.40	Recreation — Paper cutting & modelling —
2.40 – 3.30	Handwork

Empire Daisy.

Closed school at the end of afternoon session for Whitsuntide holiday (1 week).

May 31st — Reopened school this morning. 28/28 present. Denis Bagshaw re-admitted — has attended Royston Queen's Rd Council School during absence from Warkton (8th March 1920 — 21 May 1920 87/87 attendance — certified by Hd Master M.R. Hewett)

Two infants under five years of age admitted.

Miss Jackson absent from school all day.

June 1st — Mr J Turnbull — Organising Secretary of Northants Temperance & Band of Hope Union — visited this morn 9.45 – 10.45 — lectured on

1921 a detailed programme for the school children to follow on Empire Day as recorded in the school log book.

Nov. 21st   Mr Palmer visited

" 23rd   Thursday afternoons basket-
making will be taken
instead of Copy Books &
Reading (2.30 — 3.30)
Recreation on this day
will be at 2.20 instead
of 2.30 so as to give a
full hour to handwork.

Nov. 24th   Aver: Attendance 29.7.
Percentage 87.3.
Epidemic is spreading
therefore attendance is
pulled down.

Dec 1st   Average attendance 30.9
Percentage 90.8.
Attendance slightly better
this week.

Dec. 8th   Average attend: 31.9
Percentage 93.8.

November 23rd 1911. This entry in the school log book indicates that handiwork
was part of the school curriculum.

School children and the teacher Miss Drew, with some of their handiwork in 1913.

Date	Article Sold	Number Sold	Price	To Whom Sold	Amount	
No: 1911	Vests (small)	2	8½ª	Parent	1	5
July 1912	Muslin Pinafore	1	1/¼	"	1	0
"	Pett	1	8½	"		8½
"	Vest	1	10½	"		10½
C 9 9	Petticoat	1	8½	"		8½
Sept	Muslin Pinafore (large)	1	1/-	"	1	0
"	" Small	1	9ª	"		9
"	Print Pinafore	2	7ª	"	1	2
"	Pillowslips	2	6ª	"	1	0
"	"	1	6ª	"		6
"	Tea Cloths	3	5ª	"	1	3
"	Dishcloths	2	1ª	"		2·
"	Linen Apron	1	1/2	—	1	2
"	Print Pina: (small)	1	3½	"		3½
"	Pillowslips	2	6	"	1	0
"	Tea Cloths	2	5ª			10
Oct	Tea Cloths	2	5·ª	Mrs Whistler		10
"	Petticoat	1	8½	Parent		8½
"	Kettleholders	6	1½	Children		9
"	Dishcloth	1	1	"		1
"	Handkerchiefs	5	1	"		5
"	Kindergarten Articles	2	½			1
"					16	8½

May 1913 a copy of the handiwork sales book showing the type of articles that were made by the pupils and sold for school funds.

61

Nov. 22. Mixed department. = 100%
Attendance for whole School
= 32·8
Percentage for school. 99·3

Nov: 25th Fred Brown granted a
total exemption certificate
Now on Books = 32.

The following alterations have
been made in the Infant.
Timetable. (upon the advice of H. M. I.)

	A. M.	P. M.
Monday:	11 - 12	2. - 2.30
	Handwork	Claymod:
Tuesday.	10 - 10.30 Writing	1st 3.10 - 3.30 Reading
	9.40 - 10 Form & Colour	2nd Writing
	11 - 12 A.M.	2 - 2.30 Conversational
Wednesday. Inf. + Std I.	Handwork	2.30 - 3 Brushwork
		2.30 - 3 Drawing
Thursday.		3.10 - 3.35 Reading.

See Timetable in
Infant Division

Nov. 29. Percentage for week = 93·7

School children taken in 1921 outside the school building showing typical clothing for this period.

10 children.

July 21st — Average attendance for the week 15.6.
Percentage 91.1.

July 27th — Revd C. R. Norcock visited this afternoon.

28th — Average attendance for the week. 16.
Percentage 94.1

July 31st — Mr Viccars S.A.O visited this morning.

Aug 4th — Average attendance for the week 15.6.
Percentage 91.7
School closed this afternoon for
Midsummer Vacation (5 wks)
Sylvia Warren left today
She will attend The Rockingham Road
Sen. Girls' School.
Stock received from L. J. Harold & Son.

September 11th — School re-opened this morning.
29 evacuees were received into the
school.
Miss Stanners is the teacher in charge.
The total number of scholars is 44.
The children have been divided into
two classes.
Miss Stanners taking charge of

The impact of evacuees from the Christ Church School, Albany Street, London was recorded in the Log book. 29 evacuees swelled the role number by 50%. At the beginning of the bombing campaign on 14th May 1940 the children were all summoned to the school. The Kettering sirens were easily heard in the village and all children were required to carry their gas masks at all times, if a pupil came to school without their gas mask they were sent home to fetch them as it was thought that gas attacks were imminent.

A class of Warkton school children 1940. 50% of these children were evacuees from the Regents Park area of London.

Evacuees Barbara and Derick Sears who stayed at numbers 23 and 25 Warkton during the war.

In 2004 a reunion of evacuees was held in Warkton and Barbara wrote her memories of this period in her life.

(Barbara Sears could not attend but she sent the following to be read at the gathering by her brother Derek.)

MEMORIES OF WARKTON FROM EVACUEE BARBARA SEARS NOW LIVING IN AUSTRALIA.

"My first memory is of you and I walking hand in hand to Euston Station (you in a blue outfit and me in rusty brown. The children walked in file down the middle of the street and the mothers on the pavement crying.

Arriving at the 'school' in Warkton with all the other evacuees. I suppose we had luggage but only remember the brown paper bag, from I think Cadbury's, with chocolate in it.

Waiting at the school to be 'chosen' by the Toseland's. I was picked up by Arthur and Jessie with a girl who was about 14 called Jessie Flower but she did not stay with us long. I remember sleeping with her in the attic bedroom that smelled of apples and the 'big bed' that had a beautiful hand knitted patchwork bedspread.

Having baths in front of the fire downstairs. The fireplace was hung with horse brasses and the bath was a big long tin one. (We had a bath once a week I think). The same bath was kept under the stairs and during an air raid it was made into a bed which I slept in. I remember during one big raid (I suspect it was the night Coventry Cathedral was bombed and burnt out) we all stood outside somewhere and from a distance we could see the flames of Coventry burning.

The sweet shop opposite the church and the lady with whiskers who used carefully weigh out our sweet ration, bulls eyes, liquorice sausages (we used the red ones for lipstick) and sherbet lemons.

The pigs and lovely little piglets Cyril and Lily kept and the sides of bacon which used to hang from the ceiling in their cottage. They also had fresh water cress growing in their running stream.

Arthur going off on his motor bike each day to work in a munitions factory.

The hay-making times when we used to ride on top of the hay carts.

The lovely big lumbering cart horses that pulled them. Hiding and playing hide and seek in the hay stacks. The wonderful smell of the hay.

The men used to drink or eat 'sop' which was bread mixed with cold tea. We used to have gorgeous bread and dripping sandwiches.

On Sundays we always had a roast. I always sat at the end of the table on the piano stool and we always ate the Yorkshire pudding first on it's own with just gravy on it.

I always felt very cosy and safe at Jessie and Arthur's and I don't ever remember them being unkind or cross with me and we used to pick black, white and red currants together with gooseberries (which we used to suck the insides from to make little balloons) from the back garden. All the vegetables were home grown. I used to make little fairy beds from match boxes and leave them under the fruit trees for the fairies to find. Jessie told me that the little white moths that used to fly around in the daytime were really fairies at night. We also used to make little ballerinas from the fuchsia flowers that grew there. In the summer all the pergolas that joined both the Toseland houses were covered with small pink and red roses.

After the corn harvest the men would stand around the ever decreasing circle of corn with their guns and shoot the rabbits that were hiding in it and then we would have rabbit pie for dinner. Remember the song the 'Run Rabbit, run rabbit, run, run, run, don't let the farmer have his fun, fun, fun. I have never eaten rabbit since.

The wonderful snowy winters. Snowmen, snowball fights and sliding down the hills on sledges which I think were old tin trays. Chilblains that ached.

The school 'play shop' which we all loved.

The little purple flower that grew in the walls of the school and the walls that seemed so high to shut out the world.

The May-day parades, particularly the one where Alan Toseland and Rosalind Bagshaw were May King and Queen, (she had a beautiful bright pink velvet cloak which all us girls coveted.). We all carried posies of flowers and when from house to house around the village singing May songs including one "the cuckoo is a pretty bird, he singeth as he flies".

The concerts and 'dress ups' we used to play in the alleyway that led to the walk over the fields to Kettering. (a walk we loved since we had to climb over several stiles and walk through the cow tracks on the way). I think the alley way was by the farm at the back of the Toselands. We all thought we were Vera Lynn and used to sing and dance to "There'll be bluebirds over the white cliffs of Dover, tomorrow just you wait and see".

The big house (Rectory) and all the treasures and fresh peaches in the greenhouse etc. Queenie, the cook in her giant kitchen. The large tree by the back door that produced little pods that the women would wire together with long coloured beads to make brooch button holes. The pheasants being hung until they were all maggoty.

The hips and haws, hedge layering and the wonderful magical avenue of trees.

The American soldiers who used to give us gum.
Going to the fair in Kettering, the rides etc, the gypsies selling pegs.

Picking giant mushrooms (one would fill a frying pan and made lovely juice as it fried) in the fields.

Big picnics and we all went blackberrying and picked buckets and buckets of them. We all ended up with purple mouths and fingers and afterwards scrumptious blackberry and apple pies and blackberry jam to die for.

Scrumping and pinching apples from peoples gardens.

The whole school getting nits and having paraffin combed through our hair.

Nativity plays at Christmas and the special musty smell in the church and the big white statues which used to frighten us. The swallows that nested in the church porch. The smell of carnations from the flowers at funerals. The graves fascinated us.

Bertie and Pam Lumbers and the cubby we had in the hedge.

Bird nesting and collecting eggs.

Drawing faces on hens eggs at Easter.

The Harvest Festivals in the church when it was beautifully decorated with sheaves of corn etc.

The bump in the road that used to make your tummy churn when you went over it in the bus from Kettering.

Seeing my first Barrage Balloon.

Wonderful herby sausages that Alf made.

Aunty Jessie doing the washing in the copper once a week and the blue bag to make the sheets white.

Collecting wild flowers, (the smell of meadow sweet) pressing them and sticking them in a book.

Fishing for tiddlers and guppies in the stream near the bridge.

The Blacksmiths shop with all its wonders and the smell of the fire and the burning hooves when they shod the horses.

The way the country kids used to tease us because of the way we Londoners talked.

Going carol singing.

The way they put sulphur powder on wounds when we fell over.

Sucking honey out of the ends of cowslips, watching as they smoked the beehives to get the honey out.

A great feel of village life and how everyone knew everyone.

Grandpa's house (I'm not sure if this was Arthur or Jessies parents, I think Jessies) where Julia Gallagher was evacuated, with it's front room that was immaculate and polished to within an inch of its life, but was never used except for truly special occasions.

Dig for Victory signs in the Post office.

The daffodils, snowdrops and crocuses and thatched roofs, the cacti plants in Jessie and Lily's windows.

I suppose there must have been some negative things to being an evacuee kiddie but I honestly can't remember them. I only think of it as a truly wonderful experience and magical time of my life that has remained with me together with the Toseland's kindness and love all my life."

Barbara

325

The Library Van visited the school this afternoon for an exchange of books.

May 8th Visited the School this morning & signed Registers. C.R. Vincock.

May 10th Perfect attendance has been made for the fourth week in succession. School closed this mid-day for Whitsun holiday. (one week)

May 14th In consequence of the sudden crisis school re-opened this morning $\frac{19}{28}$ present. Several children are on holiday with their parents.

May 17th Average attendance for the week 23·1 Percentage 71%.

May 24th Empire Day was celebrated this morning. After taking the Salute, appropriate songs & recitations were rendered by the children. The Rev'd C.R. Horcock gave a short address & the ceremony concluded with the National Anthem. Mr Viccaro S.A.P. visited this morning. Average attendance for the week 239 Percentage 84%

Log book entry 14th May 1940
This emergency reopening of the school was on the second day of the Whitsun holiday. The message to reopen the school would have been relayed by word of mouth as at this time only two households had their own telephone,
Mr Charles Lamb who lived at the Old Rectory and Mr Donovan Lane who lived at no 19 Warkton.

Admission Number.	Date of Admission or Re-admission.	Name of Child. (Christian and Surname.)	Birth-day. (Exact date.)	Name and Address of Parent or Guardian.
Evacuees	18			
1		Emberson Edna Joyce	18	
2		Flower Jessie	18	
3		Dymond Clara Lilian	18	
4		Mizon, Lilian Kathleen	18	
5		Ade, Irene Pamela	18	
		Barr, Kathleen Mary	18	
7		Irvine, Janet Agnes	18	
8		Rainbow, Jean Florence ✓	18	
9		Marr, Margaret Winifred	18	
		Yates, Pamela, Florence ✓	18	
		Hale Marjorie Betty	18	
12		Sears, Barbara, Joan ✓	18	
13		Gallagher, Julia, Lilian ✓	18	
		Yates, Sylvia, Edith ✓	18	
15		Yates, Audrey Elsie ✗	18	
16		Marr Sheila Mary	18	
17		Rainbow, Eric, William	18	
18		Marr Robert, William	18	
19		MacDonald, Sydney	18	
20		MacDonald, Edward	18	
		Semark, Terence ✓	18	
22		Sears Derek, John ✓	18	
23		Dymond, Leonard Wm	18	
24		MacDonald, Frederick	18	
25		McGiffin Alma	30 7 1932	
26		McGiffin Eileen	26 11 1930	
27		Parker Sylvia	13 11 1933	
28		McGiffin John	14 1 1935	
29		Fennel William	14 4 1937	
15	Re-admitted	Yates Audrey Elsie		
30	30 9 40	Pyke Stanley Terence		
31	10 10 40	Pridgman Sheila M	3 9 1927	
32				

Register of evacuees in 1942.

April 27th   Av. att. for week = 15
                Percentage ..   ..   = 100%.
                As the children have made 100% attendance
                they are allowed to leave at 3.45 p.m.

30th   I admitted Marc Oliver aged four years.

May 2nd   The school closes this afternoon for the
                usual May Day holiday.

3rd   School re-opened today. 17 children present.

3rd   Mr. Jones S.A.O. visited.

4th   Av. attendance for week = 16.7
                Percentage for week = 98.5
                Rev. C. R. Norcock visited.

11th   The children have today returned to
                school after having had three days
                holiday two days being for VICTORY
                celebrations as the "cease fire" in Europe
                was announced on May 8th, and one
                day being for Ascension Day.
                Av. attendance for week = 15
                Percentage for week = 88.2

14th   Rev. C. R. Norcock visited during
                religious instruction. 17 children present.

18th   Av. attendance for week = 15.4. Percentage = 90.6

Cease fire in Europe the log book entry for May 11th 1945.

Warkton school pupils with their teacher Mrs Reynolds in 1945. Showing the steep decline in pupil numbers with the return of the evacuees to London. It was at this time that closure of the school was first muted, but it managed to stay open for a further fifteen years.

A group of children outside the school C1950

433

<u>Copy of H. M Inspector's Report</u>
<u>Inspected</u> on
14<u>th</u> <u>February</u> <u>1951.</u>

15 children of primary school age attend
this isolated village school whence they
are transferred at the age of 11+ either
to Grammar Schools or to Secondary Modern
Schools in Kettering.

Recently redecorated, the lofty classroom
provides adequate room for unrestricted
movement. A great improvement has been
effected since main water supply was
connected to these premises; a wash
basin has been installed in the lobby and
the obsolete offices converted into hygienic
water closets. The uneven grass and gravel
surface of the playground, however, seriously
limits the physical development + welfare
of the children. School meals are not
provided.

The qualified teacher in charge was appointed
to this school almost four years ago after

considerable teaching experience. Reading develops satisfactorily; a classroom library of lively and suitable books might be built up when conditions permit. Number generally is weak and the value of repetitive exercise working appears to be overstressed. The use of simple apparatus, the linking of formal work with practical experience and the organisation of progressive group oral lessons would go some way to improving the work. Composition develops slowly; a range of lively topics together with the necessary oral preparation might stimulate further interest. Geography, History and Nature Study lessons, largely confined to the text books provided, might advantageously be expanded so as to provide opportunities for adequate oral lessons and the value of informal recording of lessons by older children could profitably be considered. The art teaching is over-formal; there is little interest shown despite the more frequent use of powder paint. Broadcast

435

lessons in Music and Movement
are greatly enjoyed.
The children are friendly but
in general they appear to need
more organised oral teaching,
practical and constructional work and
the opportunity to express
themselves.   C.R Nowak. 17. IV. '51

A copy of the Inspector's report dated 14th February 1951 gives a good
insight into the school's post war progress. Pupil numbers rose in the 1950s to
a maximum of 15.

A daffodil competition held for the school children in 1954.

Children at play in 1957 in the playground outside the school.

School concert 1953

Children leaving their school for the last time. It was eventually closed at Easter 1961. This photograph shows the six remaining pupils waving "goodbye" to their teacher Miss Cottingham on the left and the school caretaker, Mrs Tilley on the right.

People

In the 17th and 18th centuries, records show that the population in the village averaged at just over 300 persons. When the national census was first undertaken in 1801, up to the year 2000, The population of Warkton varied from the highest at 316 in 1861 to the lowest 104 in 1981. Over 200 years an average of 212 people were shown as living in the parish of Warkton. The census also revealed the extent of child fatalities in the early years of the 19th century. From 1811 to 1860 there were 67 deaths, from 1861 to 1910 there were 34, and from 1911 to 1960 there were only 7 deaths. Thus showing that increased hygiene, living conditions and general health had resulted in a dramatic fall in the number of infant deaths.

Up to the First World War the vast majority of villagers were employed either on farms or on the estate, walking to their places of work. Hours were long and the work was at times physically demanding and tedious. Inspite of this, the men took time to tend their gardens growing vegetables for their families.

Quite a few Warkton children were given apprenticeships either in Kettering or Great Glen Leicestershire. The Overseer placed poor children into apprenticeships for a period of 7 years training. For example:

> 1752 John East a poor child aged 14 to William Norman Weaver Kettering.
> 1768 John Saddington aged 14 to John Tingle Millar Kettering.
> 1780 Samuel Harriet aged 14 to Mr Peters Framework Knitter Great Glen.
> 1800 Roger Burditt aged 14 to Mr Peters Framework Knitter Great Glen.
> 1802 John Osbourne aged 14 to Mr Peters Framework Knitter Great Glen.
> 1806 William Bamford aged 16 to Mr Wait Stockingframe Needlemaker Great Glen.

This served two purposes, on the one hand it gave them employment of a sort on the other it took them out of poor relief, thus saving money.

In 1870s, when Henry Stobart was the Rector at St Edmunds church, he started a reading room in the new school. In 1877 he wrote: *"the schoolroom has been opened three days of the week during the winter, from 6.30 to 9.00 pm. I regret that a larger number of an older age have not taken advantage of this means of passing with amusement or profit some part of the long evenings. For a small subscription of sixpence a month, a member can have the reading of several weekly papers, such as the Illustrated News, the Graphic, Animal World, Parish Fun, Land and Water, as well as newspapers of the County, various periodicals etc. With games of chess, draughts, dominos etc and always a roaring fire and good light"*.

Cottages in the village at this time were small, many over crowded and difficult to light adequately with candles or oil lamps, and not very warm in the dark winter evenings.

After this period more and more village residents found employment in the towns, and huge changes occurred with the advent of electricity to Warkton in 1921. Street lights were not introduced into the village until the 1960s.

Most houses had their own well for fresh water, the few that did not have a well shared with their neighbour. In the late eighteenth century, some of these wells had become polluted, by the continuous emptying of human waste into the gardens, which over time seeped into the wells, causing serious illnesses. It was then decided to tap into five springs that were situated in the fields above the village by diverting the water into a specially built reservoir.

A photograph of the reservoir

This was approximately ten foot square and built opposite the village green.
The water was piped around the village, with six stand pipes installed at strategic points. People would come and collect their water from these water taps in buckets, and take this back to be heated in their homes, either in a fire heated copper or over an open fire. This water was used for all drinking and domestic use. This system continued until 1925, when the pipes in Warkton were linked to the mains supply at Kettering. In the mid 1930s all homes were connected direct to the main supply. In 1948 bathrooms and lavatories were installed in all cottages throughout the village under a government directive. Prior to this there were only five houses with main sewerage lavatories in the village.

In the early 1930s the first telephone cable was extended to the village, with two home owners becoming connected. The public phone box was installed in the 1950s. There was a post office in Warkton in 1840 which ceased to trade in 2001. During this period it was sited in four different houses being run under licence by the lady of the house.

There was a butchers shop at number 46 which traded from 1833 until about 1900. This was run by Mr Bagshaw from Grafton Underwood. Bread was bought from the Bakehouse which started trading in 1621, and this shop also sold confectionary.

Two houses used their front rooms as a general stores, selling groceries and stationary items, these were at number 5 and number 33. The bay window at number 33 was installed at this time to display the goods for sale. All these shops declined during the 1930s with more and more deliveries coming from Kettering to the village by bicycle or van.

John Mutton. C1869 He was born in the village, and worked as a farm labourer. When he married, he moved to Burton Latimer, returning to live at Warkton in 1894, in the cottage that is now number 8, which was built in 1827.

John and Mary Ann Mutton C1900 outside the door of number 8. John's great great grandson Ian now owns this same Cottage in the village.

Edwin (Ted) John Mutton's youngest son 1890.He worked on a farm all his life including his own smallholding.

Ted Mutton with his daughter Edna at number 31, in 1921. This was a smallholding, when Ted retired from farming, The Sargeant family took over this farm with additional acreage.

Ted Mutton and family moved to number 44. Ted Mutton used to have the task of winding the Church clock on a weekly basis, and he tolled the bell to announce the death of a villager whenever this occurred. At the death knell four tolls were given for a man, three for a woman, and two for a child. The knell was tolled for ten minutes then rung for twenty minutes, the bell being half muffled. He also rang for the church services tolling three bells himself, one rope in each hand and a third with one foot. His wife Polly was the church caretaker, in 1951 her wages were five shillings per week.

Frank, John Muttons' fifth son, with his second wife Lucy. They emigrated to the USA C1910, and he later changed his surname to Myrton.

George Toseland 1898.
He moved from Grafton
Underwood to live in Warkton
at number 25 in 1904. As his
family grew, in 1910, he was
allowed to have number 24
as well to accommodate his
five children. These two
cottages were separated
back into two single dwellings in
the early 1990s.

George aged twenty and Edith
Toseland aged eighteen in 1900 on
their wedding day.

The Toseland family 1918.
Alfred. Edith. Phylis. Archie. Cyril. Arthur.

Thomas Turner and
Cyril Toseland at play
in 1912,with a goat
pulling a cart which
they used to ride in.

Cyril Toseland aged 20. He lived at number 25 for a total of 84 years. When he married Helen Mutton in 1933 he remained at number 25 and his father together with the rest of the family moved into number 45. It was at this time that George, Cyril and Alfred started farming in their own right to the rear of number 45 in what was known as The Nursery, where Osiers were grown to be planted on The Estate and elsewhere. On Armistice Day 11th November 1918 eleven poplar trees were set in the front of the nursery to commemorate the end of the Great War. Seven were blown down in a violent gale in 1947, when many large trees in the area were uprooted. To date there are two of these poplars remaining.

Edith Toseland aged 78. Cycling to Kettering to do her shopping. She did this journey two to three times a week until she was 80 years old. (5 mile round trip) 1958.

Cyril Toseland growing his tobacco
in 1948. When the leaves were big enough (2ft 6in x
1ft) they were collected, threaded on a wire, hung
up in the barn to dry, when dry they were painted
with a mixture of rum and treacle, then Cyril would
put the leaves in a press where they would be kept
for about six months to mature, then the tobacco
would be ready for cutting and used for smoking. At
that period he gave the majority of this tobacco
away to the elderly persons in the village for them
to smoke. The children of the village used to collect
coltsfoot leaves from the fields to supplement the
tobacco crop if there were insufficient tobacco
leaves for this curing process. This was not as pure
a flavour and was thus not very popular, but the
men still smoked it.

George Warren Lamb and his wife Agnes Anne. C1870s. Agnes was the youngest daughter of Doctor Roughton of Kettering. Their son Frederick, held the posts of County Court Registrar, and Clerk to the Justices. He died in 1901 aged 44 years.

FRIDAY, JANUARY 22, 1915.

A Kettering Worthy.

Lamented Death of Mr. George W. Lamb.

THE LATE MR. G. W. LAMB.

George Warren Lamb born in 1828. He was a partner in a legal practice which is now Lamb and Holmes, it was established by his father Henry Wortley Lamb in 1813. He retired from this post in 1893, becoming tenant of a smallholding at the Glebe Farm Warkton; a smallholding of about thirty seven acres: which he farmed until 1898 when he sold up and retired to Hove, Brighton. He was Chairman of the Warkton Parish meeting from 1894 to 1897. He was buried in St Edmunds Churchyard Warkton in 1915 aged 86.

154

Charles Edward Lamb 1930. He bought The Rectory in 1921 when the living of Warkton was combined with that of Weekley and the clergyman for both villages lived in the Weekley vicarage. This picture was taken outside his front door. He cycled daily to work in Kettering with his lunch box strapped to the handle bars. Charles Lamb was a partner in the Lamb and Holmes practice and was Clerk to the Justices and County Court Registrar.

Alice Lamb wife of Charles. She worked tirelessly for the benefit of the village and hosted the village fete in the grounds of her home at the Old Rectory for many years

John Lamb and his wife Margot in 1983. She was a stalwart of the Warkton Village Hall Committee and the Women's Institute, being on the County Executive for many years and a long serving member of the Mother's Union and St Edmunds Church Choir. John lived at the former Rectory, following the death of his father with Margot and their six children. John Lamb was a Solicitor with the firm of

Lamb and Holmes established by his great grandfather, Henry Lamb in 1813. He was Chairman of the Local Appeal Tribunal and Clerk to The Justices for 20 years. He was also Chairman of the Warkton Parish Meeting. John was awared a Silver Jubilee Medal in 1977.

Florence Lamb C1925. Daughter of Charles and Alice. She was a qualified musician, organised the choir and was an active participant in Weekley and Warkton Women's Institute. She was an enthusiastic beekeeper. During the Second World War, she was a member of The Voluntary Aid Detachment, nursing in hospitals. She was greatly involved in Warkton village life until she married Sub Lieutenant Bill Patterson in 1948 and moved to Essex.

A daughter of the Rev Alfred James Whistler (1910 - 1920) outside the Rectory.

Owen and Ellen Henson. She is knitting socks for soldiers in the Great War 1915 and Owen is sawing fire wood for the home. Most women knitted comforts for the men in the war.

Hannah Henson C1880. She moved from Grafton Underwood to Warkton when her husband died to be with her brother in law Charlie Henson and his wife at number 15.

Charlie and Harriet Henson they lived at no 15. Charlie was a hedger and ditcher for Boughton Estate. Charlie was born in Grafton Underwood and worked at Overstone in the Great War, moving to Warkton Lodge in 1918, and to number 15 Warkton in 1930.

Charlie bringing home produce from his allotment. As he was lame, he could only use one hand to pull his truck, with a stick in the other and thus used a rope over his shoulder attached to the other handle to balance the truck.

Charlie with his produce of Onions in 1950. (note the chickens in the run. Most villagers kept a few chickens and some also had a pig.)

Cecil Clifford. 1912. His family moved from Orton to Warkton in the 1870s.

He worked at Mobbs and Lewis, last makers in Kettering almost all his life. He cycled to work every day, a good two miles each way, always returning home for his lunch.

The Turner family C1895, with the Rector in their front garden. Isebrook Farm was situated at the south west corner of the village.

C1910. The Turner family Mary. Amy. Thomas. Arthur. George with the dog Trissie.
Note that the start of the Kettering footpath is at the right hand side of the picture.

Henry Knights' children. 1895. Cecil. Henry. Nellie. And the youngest son Philip, who was killed in the Great War.
The Knights farmed The Firs (now known as Moorfield) in Warkton.

Harry Tilley C 1910. He lived at number 1. Harry was injured in the Great War. When he returned home from the front, he went to work in Poulton's shoe factory in Kettering, moving to Wilson and Watson, where he became a foreman.
However he never really got over his war injuries and died in March 1938 aged forty eight.

Bert Taylor C1920. Lived at number 22. He lost his left arm having been gored by a bull on Dunkley's farm.

Ada Collins with her nephew Roy outside
number 20. 1933.

Mr and Mrs West with John
Braybrook September 1914,
outside number 43. Mr West was
a roofer for Boughton Estates.

Mr and Mrs Gillings in the front garden of number 35, with number 33 in the background. Mr Gillings worked in the Estate office. During his working life, on The Estate, Mr Gillings and family lived in seven

different cottages in the village.

Mr and Mrs Gillings celebrating their golden wedding November 1928.

Photo   S. Percival.

MR. JOHN FLETCHER,

John Fletcher gamekeeper November 1909. His family moved from Clitheroe, Lancashire, to be gamekeepers on the estate, in 1804 and they lived in the now number 45 Warkton. The third generation of the family remained there until John died in Weekley Hospital in 1933, a total of almost one hundred and thirty years.

Burt Wadsworth and his wife outside number 45, in 1935 showing Cyril Toseland's Austin car and part of the huge walnut tree that stood at the rear of number 46 that was felled in 1959.

165

Mr. C. Dunkley, C.C., a well-known farmer, of Warkton.

Mr C Dunkley.
County
Councillor.
He farmed at the
Firs after the
Knights left the
village in 1910.

Three road men outside
Kettering Hospital in
March 1862.
Ezra Mutton of Warkton is on
the right of the picture.

John Goodman C1890. He was an agricultural labourer who worked on various farms all his life in Warkton. Part of a tribute to him at his funeral in May 1905 *"John was a true specimen of an English agriculturalist, now alas growing so scarce. Strong, handsome and lovable. He lives again in his children who respect his memory"*. Two of his sons were Sergeant Majors in the Royal Marine Artillery.

Lewis and Eliza Goodman 1938. He was a gardener at Boughton House, and looked after St Edmunds churchyard in Warkton, he moved to number 46 in the 1880s when the houses sited behind number 12, were demolished due to their unfit state. Lewis Goodman used to sell hens eggs to the villagers and on a Saturday afternoon people would go to him to buy their weekly supply of eggs.

Ernest Goodman. William Baughan. Harold Goodman pictured at the rear of number 46 in May 1914. On the occasion of William marrying Ernest and Harold's sister.

Charlotte James with her daughter Alice and husband Lewis in 1905. Lewis was the village blacksmith for many years. This family lived at number 32.

Cissie and William
James, elder children
of Charlotte and Lewis
1885.

1950. Arthur Bliss
blacksmith at work at
the forge in Warkton.

Smithy's Forge is Art Studio

Example of His Craftsmanship

HE FASHIONS IN WROUGHT IRON

A VILLAGE smith is not always solely of the sinewy hand and iron-muscled variety. Sometimes he is an artist with a touch as fine as that of a miniature painter—like Mr. Arthur Bliss, of Warkton, for example.

This week Mr. Bliss was helping the battle for food by fixing broken harvest equipment, but quietly ticking on the mantelpiece of his home next to the smithy was a clock that tells a different story.

It is a delightful piece of artistry-in wrought iron, ornamented with an elegant design that keeps most visitors spellbound until they get around to trying to buy it.

"But I won't sell that one," says Mr. Bliss, "the wife is very fond of it, so how could I?"

From which you gather that this is not the only wrought iron clock that Mr. Bliss has made. It is not. He has made and sold many more, along with wrought iron firescreens and gates, all of them individual designs.

One magnificent pair of gates was for a famous member of the peerage, and others have gone to big houses in many parts of the country.

Own Style

"Lots of people ask me whether there is any fear of any of my work being duplicated," he says, "but there is no fear of that. All my designs are individual, done specially for the people who commission them."

One example of Mr. Bliss's work in Kettering is in the garden of Coun. A. E. Munn. It is a gate leading through from the lawn to the fish-

THIS elegant wrought iron clock is an outstanding example of the craftsmanship of Mr. Arthur Bliss. This is the only one of the many he has fashioned he has not

TURNING from his forge at Warkton is Mr. Arthur Bliss, whose work in wrought iron is reputed for its artistry.

Arthur Bliss at work in the 1950s.

Duncan Dalziel, farrier and blacksmith creating wrought iron work C1965. He worked for forty years following the trade of his father and grandfather who were blacksmiths in Scotland. After being demobbed from the RAF he came to live at the gatehouse at Boughton and worked for Arthur Bliss, taking over the business upon the death of Arthur, and moved to number 32 Warkton.

170

1906 Showing the wheelwright working with Lewis James. They are putting the iron rim on a wooden wheel, outside the blacksmiths' shop.

The blacksmith shop C1975. There has been a Smithy in the village for over three hundred years though not always in the same building. It was originally opposite the Bakehouse moving to its' present position in the 1870s. The far end of the building is the location of the previous picture (the wheelwright)

Horses waiting to be shod outside the blacksmiths' shop in the 1960s. At one
time there were two and sometimes three blacksmiths shoeing up to eighty horses
per week. Until the 1950s a blacksmith would travel from Warkton to Grafton
Underwood every Tuesday to shoe horses there. Heavy and light horses
were brought to the farrier from as far away as Tywell, Rushton and of
course Kettering.

The blacksmiths also undertook repairs to agricultural implements and household
wares, as well as the production of simple tools, latches, bolts, nails etc. In 1927
they made a new weather vane for the stable block at Boughton House which is
still in situ to date. They even travelled as far away as Rockingham for in 1927,
Cyril Toseland and Arthur Bliss went to Rockingham Castle where in the grounds
there was a deep well. And at that time Rockingham Estates had to draw water out
using a bucket, as was usual. But they wanted to use a mechanical pump instead.
The pump that was available was inadequate for the job, the blacksmith's brief
was to climb into the well and fix the pump to the wall just above the water line so
that it could extract the water. This was completed and apparently it worked, but it
was a dangerous and difficult job.

George Bagshaw senior working in the estate carpenters shop at Boughton House in 1880, he worked there all his life.

George Clarke carpenter working in the estate workshops at Weekley in 1960.

Henry Taylor and Alice 1911. They lived at number 17 Warkton. Henry was Horseman at Boughton for most of his working life, starting work at the tannery. Like most people working with animals, he never had any time off which even included working on Christmas Day and all the other feast days. For some reason even if there were two or more men attending to the animals on a farm they would all have to turn up for work. The practice of covering for each other was not permitted with the exception of a worker requiring to attend a funeral.

Roseanna Bagshaw C1890 She lived at number 33 and was in service at Frencham in Surrey, where she tragically died in a fire whilst saving two children.
She got the children to safety but sadly she died of the burns that she received.

The Bagshaw family in 1925. Alec with his father George on the right and his Grandfather, also named George on his left.

Emma Mutton 1880 She was a lacemaker, working from home.

Matilda Mutton she was a domestic servant C1890 aged 40 yrs. At one time she worked at Boughton House, and then she moved to work at the Rectory for the Rev Bridges' family.

Rennie Mutton she was a domestic servant, laundress, cook and lacemaker during her working life.

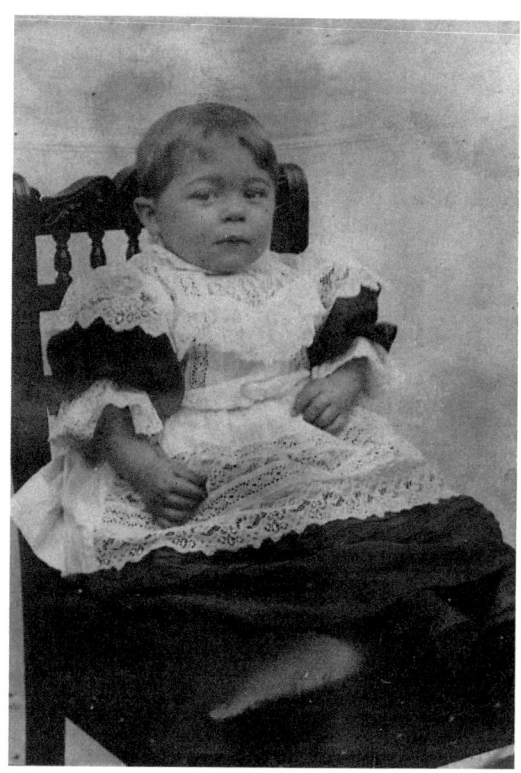

Ernest Maule aged 18 months in 1899, he was the son of Rennie Mutton. When he grew up he became a steel welder.

Hilda Maule aged 8, 1909 daughter of Rennie Mutton, she became a shoe packer, working in Kettering.

A birthday celebration for the McCormick family in 1984

Dr McCormick and Dr Willis in 1984. Taking a ride around the village with their vintage steam engine.

Crime and Punishment

The earliest known crime documented that relates to Warkton was in the year 1202 when Geodfrey of Warkton was hanged for the murder of Roger the Reaper:

Taken from the Kettering Assize Role 1202 (translated from Latin)

"Roger the Reaper was killed and Geodfrey of Warkton was taken for that death and acknowledging the death was hanged, his chattels were 12 s 0d. Wherefore Simon of Pattishall, the Sheriff ought to answer therein. William, son of Ralf, one of the jurors in mercy for default."

The next recorded offence was on October 1610 when Francis Sanders was accused of taking corn to the wrong mill, (anyone with corn to be ground was obliged by law to take it to the mill as directed by the Lord of the Manor) he was fined 3s 4d which was a huge fine for those days. In October 1789, Edward Panther a shepherd of Warkton was summoned for an assault, and in March 1790 Hannah Marriott of Kettering was accused of damaging a hedge in Warkton. There is no record of the outcomes from these two crimes.

The only time any mention of village stocks has been found is in the year 1802, when William Brampton of Warkton put in a bill for the stocks, which also included a coffin for "Coals" child. £2.7s.6d. (In today's value this would be at least £70.) So as well as the coffin it would be safe to assume that these would be new stocks.

There is a record dated 1809 of John Allan of Warkton appearing before the Justices in Northampton, nothing is mentioned about his crime, but he spent at least the next eight years in prison, five years in Northampton jail and three in Bedford. Over the eight years, there are various records relating to the supply of bread, clothing and maintenance for John Allan.

Weekley and Warkton Association for the Prosecution of Felons was formed on the first of January 1816.

WEEKLEY, WARKTON, KETTERING & DISTRICT ASSOCIATION FOR THE PROSECUTION OF FELONS

Felons Associations were founded in the period 1770 to 1830 when lawlessness in England was rampant. It was the time of the Industrial Revolution, a time of great unrest and disturbance of the traditional way of life in the country, which was changing rapidly from a rural to an urban economy. The old customs by which some sort of law and order had been maintained in England were breaking down and the current Police system had not been developed.

An extract from the article on Police in Encyclopaedia Britannica summed up the position clearly:

"In spit of repressive measures, until the end of the 18th Century the conditions alike of London and the Provinces were deplorable. Robbery and violence were rampant everywhere. Highwaymen infested the roads, footpads lurked in the streets, whilst, but too often, both watchmen and innkeepers were accessories to the commission of crime. At the commencement of the 19th Century it was computed that there was one criminal to every 22 of the population. Such was the state of affairs when in 1829 Sir Robert Peel laid the foundation of that organisation on which is based the existing Metropolitan Police System. Subsequent Acts of Parliament extended the system throughout Great Britain. Statutes passed in 1839 and 1840 permitted the formation of a paid County Police to be appointed by the Justices of the Peace for the County. The Police Act 1856 made the existence of an adequate force compulsory throughout England and Wales."

The first report of the Constabulary Force Commissioners dated March 1839 referred to the following:

"We could not adduce a stronger proof of the prostrate condition of the penal administration of the country than the great extent of the associations for self-protection to do that which it is the business of a Government to do. From the information we have received it appears that there are upwards of 500 voluntary associations for promoting the apprehension and prosecution of felons, besides very numerous voluntary associations in various parts of the country for the repression of vagrancy and mendacity. Amongst the rules of some of these associations for self-protection we find rules for mutual insurance by the payment of a part of the loss sustained by depredation: in several of the farmers' associations are rules binding the members, in the case of horse stealing, to take horse and join in pursuit of thieves upon alarm of a theft having been committed. Hereafter such associations and such rules may be cited to prove that the community in which they arose was relapsing into a state of barbarism."

The Weekley Warkton Association was formed in 1816 when provisional rules were drawn up and then finally adopted at an annual meeting held at The Montague Arms, Weekley on 3rd January 1820. The present day rules revised at the annual meeting of the Association on 27th January 1913 were much on the lines of the original rules and set out the system of cautionary notices (Rule 4) and rewards (Rule 7).

180

The accounts of the first dinner held on 6th January 1817 showed the following payments:

	£	s	d
Mr Knowles for 19 Dinners at 2 shillings each	1	18	0
Ditto for 5 Tankards of Ale	0	2	6
Ditto profit on 15 shillings worth of Liquors	0	5	0
Pipes, Tobacco, Fire, and Servant	0	7	6

An example of a cautionary notice relating to Warkton refers to the premises of Mr A Donovan Lane who lived at 19 Warkton.

The first rules of the Association provided that Mr Lamb at Kettering be Treasurer and Solicitor to this Association and to the present day that has continued to be the case. Mr Lamb's business accounts refer interestingly in the early days to the payment of toll bars, eg. to Rowell or Cranford at 6d.

Kettering was joined in the Association in 1869. Other Associations thought still to be in existence appear in the list. The local Associations for Cranford and Broughton & Cransley are no longer in existence.

The present day membership of the Association numbers 157 and rewards members of the public who have assisted the Police in cases leading to prosecution.

An introduction to the "Prosecution of felons"
Formed to try to combat incidents of rural crime by businessmen and landowners

OFFENCES	REWARDS		
	£	s.	d.
Wilfully setting fire to any House, Warehouse, Office, Workshop, Outhouse, Barn or Stable, Stack or Rick of Corn, Hay, Straw or Bark, or to any Stack of Wood, Furze, or other Fuel	10	10	0
Burglary	5	5	0
Highway Robbery	5	5	0
Stealing or Maiming any Horse, Mare, Gelding, or Ass, Ox, Cow, Calf or other Cattle, Sheep, Lambs or Pigs	5	5	0
Breaking and entering any Warehouse, Office, Workshop, Barn, Granary, or other Outhouse or Building detached from a dwelling house, with intent to steal, or stealing therefrom ...	3	3	0
Buying or receiving any Stock, Goods or Effects, the Property of a Subscriber, knowing the same to have been stolen...	3	3	0
Obtaining Money or Goods by False Pretences	3	3	0
Larceny not otherwise specified	2	2	0
Cutting down, Barking or wantonly Damaging Trees, Underwood, or Quicksets growing	2	2	0
Dogs worrying Cattle or Sheep	2	2	0
Robbing or Maliciously Damaging any Garden, Orchard or Fishpond	1	1	0
Stealing, or Maliciously Killing Poultry or Dogs	1	1	0
Stealing Corn or Grain, unthrashed, or Hay out of any Barn, or from any Rick or Hovel, or any Grass or Hay, growing, or in Shocks or Cocks ...	1	1	0
Stealing or Damaging any Waggon, Cart, Plough or other Implement of Husbandry	1	1	0
Breaking, Stealing, or Damaging any Hedge, Hurdle, or Tray, or Stealing Firewood, or any Gate, Post, Rail, Pale, Fence or any Ironwork belonging thereto	1	1	0
Wilful Damage to Walls, Buildings or any Property of any Member or Associate not included in preceding offences	1	1	0
Cruelty to Animals	1	1	0
Cutting the Manes or Tails of Horses, Mares, or Geldings, or the Tails of Bulls, Oxen, or Cows, or otherwise disfiguring them, or stealing Wool from Sheep, or Milk from Cows	1		0
Stealing Turnips, Green Peas, or any vegetables from the fields	0	10	0

And for every other offence, not before specified, such reward as the Committee shall think proper. ...

A list of offences and rewards appertaining to rural crime drawn up by the committee of the Felons Association. The rewards to be paid to any persons who are not members of the association who shall give evidence that shall lead to the conviction of offenders.

182

INSTRUCTIONS

BE ATTENDED TO.

I. That a place of Meeting be appointed in each Parish, by the Inspectors, for the Horse Patrol and Special Constables to assemble, in case of alarm.

II. In the event of an alarm of Fire, or any disturbance or riotous Assemblage taking place during the night, the Watch is instantly to apprise the Inspector of his Parish, who is to call first upon his Horse Patrol, and immediately to forward one of them to the Inspector of Kettering, and another to the Inspector of the nearest adjoining Parish, who will, in like manner, forward one of his Horse Patrol to the next Parish, and so through the different Parishes comprised in the District, till the whole are made acquainted with the circumstance.

III. Each Inspector then to call upon all, or such a number of the Special Constables of his Parish as he may think proper, in order that they may directly meet at the appointed places in their respective Parishes, and from thence proceed with such a force of Horse Patrol and Special Constables, as can be spared from his own Parish, towards the place where a disturbance or riotous Assemblage is ascertained to be.

IV. One influential Person, at least, to remain in each Parish, to have the charge of those Special Constables left for the protection of his Parish.

V. The Inspectors, and the influential Persons of each Parish, are recommended to keep their Special Constables as much together as possible, and to form a junction with the force from other Parishes, before an attempt is made to disperse the Rioters, should such Rioters be much more numerous than the special Constables.

OBSERVE :—It is not necessary that the Constables should wait for the arrival of a Magistrate, before they proceed to suppress riot or tumult.

The Inspectors are requested to attend at the Committee Meeting on Friday, the 17th of December, 1830, with an Account of the Expenses they have incurred, that they may be examined and paid. The Committee will sit for this purpose every alternate Friday.

Dash, Printer, Market Place, Kettering.

Instructions for Horse Patrols issued in December 1830.

KETTERING
DISTRICT ASSOCIATION,
FOR THE PROTECTION OF PROPERTY.

THE FOLLOWING IS
A LIST OF THE PARISHES COMPRISED IN THE DISTRICT;
THE NAMES OF THE INSPECTORS IN EACH PARISH;
AND THE NUMBER OF HORSE PATROL WHICH WILL BE PROVIDED BY SUCH PARISHES.

PARISHES.	INSPECTORS.	No. of HORSE PATROL.
Kettering	Mr. W. Cook, *Horse P.* / Mr. W. Roberts *Foot.* / Mr. J. D. Gotch	30
Barton Seagrave	Captain Stopford	8
Burton Lattimer	Mr. John Eady	8
Isham	Mr. S. Pulver	4
Orlingbury	Newton Young, Esq.	5
Pytchley	Henry Hensman, Esq.	8
Broughton	Charles Morris, Esq.	14
Finedon	Mr. William Leete / Mr. Robert Smith	12
Cransley	William Rose, Esq.	7
Loddington	Admiral Eyles	6
Thorpe Malsor	John Young, Esq.	8
Rowell	Mr. Hafford	12
Desborough	Mr. Cave	
Glendon	John Booth, Esq.	3
Rushton	Mr. Ashby	7
Great Oakley	Sir Arthur Brooke, Bart.	4
Little Oakley	Mr. Knibb	4
Newton	Mr Bagshaw	4
Geddington	Lord Viscount Stopford	8
Weekley	Mr. O. Edmonds	4
Warkton	Mr. George Panther	4
Grafton	Mr. Thomas Jones	5
Orton		

The Inspectors are most earnestly recommended to give the strongest injunctions to those of the Horse Patrol who are supplied with Sabres, to make as little display of them as possible; and, in the event of riot, not to use them, except in cases of the most urgent necessity, or of self defence.

A list of parishes covered by the Kettering District Association, Inspectors and number of daily Horse Patrols.

184

Public Notice.

The following Facts ought to be known
by every Person, and are published, in order
that no one may be ignorant of the dreadful
Consequences of listening to, or uniting with,
wicked Men, for the Destruction of Property.

IF any Person shall unlawfully and maliciously set Fire to any House,
Stable, Coachhouse, Warehouse, Office, Shop, Mill, Malthouse, Barn, or
Granary; or to any Building used in carrying on any Trade, every such
Offender shall be

Guilty of FELONY, and being Convicted thereof, shall suffer DEATH as a FELON.

IF any Persons riotously and tumultuously assembled together, to the
Disturbance of the Public Peace, shall unlawfully, and with Force, destroy
any House, Stable, Coachhouse, Outhouse, Warehouse, Office, Shop, Mill,
Malthouse, Barn, or Granary; or any Building used in carrying on any
Trade or Manufactory; or any Machinery; every such Offender shall be
GUILTY of FELONY, and being Convicted thereof, shall suffer DEATH
as a FELON.

IF any Person shall unlawfully and maliciously set Fire to any Stack
of Corn, Grain, Pulse, Straw, Hay, or Wood, every such Offender shall be
GUILTY of FELONY, and being Convicted thereof shall suffer DEATH
as a FELON.

PRINTED BY ORDER OF THE KETTERING DISTRICT ASSOCIATION FOR PROTECTION
OF PROPERTY.

[DASH, PRINTER, KETTERING.]

A public notice referring to acts of felony/arson.
(Although this notice is not dated it is likely that it was displayed in the local area in 1865 after
arson attacks on properties by persons who were opposed to more and more mechanisation
being introduced into the workplace and the perceived possibility of losing their livelihoods.
This included the tannery at Warkton when the heaps of oak bark used in the tanning process were
deliberately set alight in that year.)

Weekley, Warkton, Kettering and District

ASSOCIATION.

ONE GUINEA
REWARD

NOTICE IS HEREBY GIVEN that any person or persons found stealing the produce from the Orchard of Mr. A. Donovan Lane at Warkton or damaging the Walls or Fences thereof or committing any other acts of damage to or depredation upon his property will be prosecuted.

AND NOTICE IS ALSO GIVEN that any person (not implicated) giving such information as shall lead to the conviction of the offender or offenders shall, upon such conviction, receive the above reward.

LAMB & HOLMES,
Solicitors to the Association.

KETTERING,
21st July, 1944

Printed by H. Richardson, Water Street, Kettering

A reward notice concerning the theft of produce from an orchard in Warkton, as late as July 1944.

Weekley and Warkton Felons Meeting January 1939. Charles Lamb is seated on the right.

There are 33 Associations that still meet in England, the oldest being Wellingborough formed in 1781 to Coundon (Durham) formed in 1854.

After 1894 when Kettering produced a weekly newspaper, most crimes were recorded. From then until 1946 there are three hundred and two offences reported for the parish of Warkton. All of the following crimes took place in the parish of Warkton or on the border, especially in the cases of illegal fishing where the river Ise is the boundary. There were seven cases in which Warkton persons were charged for offences that took place outside the parish. Warkton residents were charged with committing twenty two offences in the parish itself.

There were ninety charges made for game trespass of one type or another. One notorious person was charged for poaching and assault on gamekeepers who at one count had sixty seven offences against him of which thirty two were committed in Warkton Parish. Punishment was given in the form of fines ranging from five shillings to three pounds and terms of imprisonment from one week to three months with hard labour. His criminal offences appeared to cease in September 1914, one might assume that he was enlisted to fight in the First World War.

There were forty three indictments for damaging growing grass, five for damaging corn, in one case only thirteen ears of wheat. Twenty six for stealing mushrooms, twenty nine for damaging hedges or fences, five for stealing walnuts, six for illegal fishing, and three for attempted murder. The remaining cases were miscellaneous charges ranging from, not sending children to school to traffic offences.

It is interesting to note that a large percentage of the people caught poaching were also charged for other offences, i.e. stealing mushrooms, walnuts and the like, though not necessarily in Warkton parish. A few travelled quite a distance by bicycle to poach or steal.

These are only a record of the people who were apprehended and charged, there must have been numerous offences that were not detected particularly in the case of growing grass etc.

Four examples of child fines in Warkton.
In June 1900, a young girl was summoned for damaging growing grass, value one shilling, she said that she was only picking a few dog daisies, she was fined one shilling, four shillings costs with a shilling damages.
In August 1902, two school boys were convicted of wilful damage to thirteen ears of growing wheat, to the value of six pence. They were fined two shillings and three pence each.
In the same month three youths were summoned for doing damage to a fence to the value of a shilling. They said they were collecting crab apples, they were fined one shilling and eight pence each.
In June 1903, two young girls were summoned for damaging grass, value one shilling. They were picking wild flowers and were fined three shillings and sixpence each.
(when farmers were earning less that eight shillings per week , these were huge fines for the families to pay)

To try to combat rural crime mostly of a paltry nature such as walking in growing grass, stealing mushrooms etc, a policeman by the name of Lane was appointed to cover the villages of Weekley and Warkton together with Boughton Estate. He was stationed at Boughton House and it was he who apprehended and arrested most of the people linked to the crimes mentioned from 1898 to 1912 After this date the Geddington or Burton Latimer constables covered this area.

The first known recorded case that he took before the courts was in June 1899 when he alleged that a lad named George Henson was doing wilful damage to growing grass to the value of one shilling. The case was dismissed due to lack of evidence, but at the same court he summoned two men on a like offence. They pleaded guilty and were fined five shillings with three shillings cost each.
In August 1904 he saw a man and his wife picking mushrooms valued three pence. They were fined one shilling with five shillings costs. In June 1906, he saw a man gathering mushrooms to the value of two shillings. He was fined one shilling and six pence with six shillings costs, in default seven days hard labour.
His last recorded case was in August 1912 when he convicted two men of damaging a fence, to the value of a shilling. They were fined seven shillings and seven pence each.
In June 1930 fourteen courting couples were caught laying in growing grass. Four couples were taken to court and fined seven shillings and six pence each, and one couple who refused to give their names to the constable were fined fifteen shillings each.

Statistics of occupations in Warkton 1851 and 1891

This comparative list illustrates the variety of occupations to be found in the village as well as the numbers employed in the various trades. It is interesting to note the women's occupations, as well as the reference to the scholars.

Occupations for Men	1851	1891
Farmers	4	8
Farm Labourers	56	41
Graziers	2	
Shepherds	2	2
Dairymen		2
Farm Bailiffs		2
Plough Boys	2	
Cattle Dealers	2	
Gamekeepers	2	2
Mole Catcher	1	
Gardeners	1	2
Foresters		2
Woodsmen		1
Wood Carters	2	
Grooms		2
Coachman		1
Blacksmiths	2	3
Farrier		1
Carpenters	5	3
Sawyer		1
Bricklayer		1
Bricklayer's Labourers		4
Tanners	10	
Bark Cleaner	1	
Curriers	1	3

	1851	1891
Painter		1
Shoemakers	5	3
Boot Sizer		1
Shoe Riveter		1
Silk Weaver		1
Carter		1
Engineer	1	
Victualler	1	
Butcher	1	
Bakers	2	1
Errand Boy	1	1
Rector	1	1
Apprentices		3

Occupations for Women	1851	1891
Lacemakers	17	
Servants	8	12
Housekeepers	2	5
Charwomen	2	
Washerwomen		1
Launderess	1	1
Sewer		1
Dressmakers	1	3
Stay Stitcher	1	
Seamstresses	1	
School Mistresses	2	2

Farm labourers are by far the largest group of men, it is in fact 50% of the total workforce at these dates.

In 1851 Lacemakers was about 50%, although some of these worked at home, the majority would have worked in Kettering. This also applied to the shoemakers and associated trades. There are no lacemakers recorded in 1891, as by than the industry had almost disappeared in this county. There were no tanners in 1891 as the tanners had ceased trading by this date, nor a butcher as this shop had closed by then.

There were apprentices from Warkton in 1851 but they lodged away at their place of work. Most were either in Kettering or Leicester where they were learning their trade.

Paupers	6	

There were no paupers in 1891 as they were sent to the workhouse in Kettering by this time.

Not included in the above lists are wives, children under four years, the infirm, or elderly who were looked after by their own families. There were approximately six people who lived by their own means.

Scholars	1851	1891
Boys 3-8 yrs	15	7
Boys 6-16 yrs	7	15
Girls 3-8 yrs	19	20
Girls 9-16 yrs	14	13
Total	**55**	**55**

In 1851 children up to the age of 8 years of age were taught in Warkton, over this age they either went to Weekley or Kettering. By 1891, all these children attended the new Warkton School.

Customs

and

Pastimes

For many centuries games had been played between neighbouring villages, especially on feast days. The earliest known competitions were with the long bow, when Henry V111 decreed that every man should be able to use the bow with great accuracy. Those that were able were required to practice the art at every spare moment, and challenges were thrown out to other villages. Until the turn of the last century, Warkton competed mostly with Grafton, in tournaments which included cricket, football, tug of war, and bare knuckle fighting. George Toseland used to relate that as a lad, on many occasions he, together with friends watched these fights which would continue until one of the contestants was completely disabled. Some of these fights went on for many hours. Although these contests were usually of a friendly nature some of the inter-village rivalry got out of hand and fighting sometimes occurred.

This is perhaps why in the late 1890s, Warkton and Grafton tended not to compete with each other. Grafton teamed with Cranford and Warkton with Weekley. Up until that period, Weekley always teamed up with Little Oakley, but that ceased perhaps for the same reason. So Weekley and Warkton got together which is still the same today.

There were also fetes, fancy dress contests singing and local sports for children. May Day was also a special occasion which has been celebrated since the sixteenth century. On Plough Monday, the nearest Monday to January 6th, a plough boy would go round the village asking for " a penny for the plough boy", the last boy to do this in Warkton, was Tim Issitt in the 1890s. Warkton Feast, which was held on Whit Sunday, was another occasion when friends and relatives from Kettering and surrounding villages came to visit and dine. Some would partake in games while the elder people watched and generally enjoyed the day. From the 1880s an annual Horticultural Show was held in Boughton Park when Weekley and Warkton would compete as to who could present the best flowers, vegetables, jams and cakes etc. Gardens in the two villages were judged for their variety and display of cultivated plants and vegetables.

Another excuse for merry making was November 5th, Guy Fawkes Day, when a communal bonfire with a guy on the top was lit, usually in the Playcroft, when children and adults alike would gather to watch the fireworks. These unlike today, were a few fire crackers and some meek bangers, but great fun was had by all watching the guy burn.

Amateur Dramatics played a big part in the village social life, when members of the drama group from Weekley and Warkton, put on plays on an annual basis. These were held in Weekley Village Hall which was full to overflowing with admiring spectators.

Up until 1874, as with all the Estate Villages, Warkton had a Public House called the Dukes Arms, where people could go and enjoy a drink and possibly to try and forget the hardships of life. In 1874, according to witnesses of the time, a tragedy occurred, concerning a lady who went to the pub for a drink taking along a baby in its perambulator. She left the baby in the pram and went inside, where she partook of a considerable quantity of alcoholic liquor. In the mean time, a loose pig in the yard, tipped the pram over and killed the baby. The pub was immediately closed, never to open again. After this happened an outdoor beer house was set up at number twelve, which incidentally was the village laundry at this time. Beer or spirits could not be drunk on the premises. In 1913, a club was opened for men only in a building adjacent to the blacksmiths shop.

Funeral.

1933 A photograph taken at the funeral of Mr Dunkley
Mr Dunkley was an Alderman on Kettering Rural District Council, and farmed at Moorfield Farm. A typical village funeral cortège, showing a horse drawn farm cart and coffin with the mourners following behind towards the church.

A wedding group outside number 32. 1905.
The photograph is showing the wedding of the blacksmith's daughter Cissie James to John Crick, and the typical formal dress code of this period.

May 1914 Florence Goodman's wedding party at the rear of number 46.
At this time most weddings were conducted on a Sunday as it was customary for adults to work for six days a week. The ladder hanging on the wall was still there in 1999. This also shows the brick part of the house which was the rear of the butchers shop.

194

The wedding of Jessie Henson and Arthur Toseland and their principal guests
These two photographs illustrate the dress of the early 1930s. These pictures were taken outside number 45 in September 1933.

(left) Warkton Mothers Union banner dedication 1955, at St Marys' Kettering. The Mothers Union in Warkton commenced in November 1923 and disbanded in December 1989.

(below) Warkton and Weekley Mothers' Union outing to Matlock in the 1950s This was a popular annual event visiting different locations each year. These outings were usually to a Norfolk coastal resort such as Hunstanton and Cromer, leaving in the early morning and returning after dark in the evening.

A picture of Weekley and Warkton's Women's Institute C1938 taken outside Warkton School.

This was one of their many successes singing in the Mid-Northants Musical Competition, under the guidance of Florence Lamb. The Institute flourished in the two villages from 1915 until the 1970s, meeting at Warkton on alternate months.

WI market stall

MEMBERS of the Northamptonshire Federation of Women's Institutes held a charity market stall at Wellingborough, when they sold preserves, vegetables, bedding plants and crafts. Pictured above from left to right are Mrs. Margot Aspinal and Mrs. Margot Lamb, executive members, and county chairman Mrs. Mary Bowler.

Members of the Northants Women's Institute at a charity stall in Wellingborough. Mrs Margot Lamb in the centre of the picture, taken in the 1960s.

A picture taken of the Old Folks Outing in 1955.
A Warkton and Weekley committee organised an annual outing for the elderly village residents. In this photograph they are about to depart in a charabanc to Hunstanton.

The Tea Party in 1955.
Teas was served to the Old Folks upon their return from Hunstanton in Weekley Village hall.

May Day celebrated in 1921
Frank Thorley and Freda Sargeant as May King and Queen.
May Day was an annual celebration by the village children. The earliest
known record relating to Warkton May Day celebrations is in 1854.

1938. Gordon Taffs and Margaret Turner were the King and Queen. This
photograph records the May Day procession upon it's arrival at Boughton
House where Queen Mary came out to talk to the children.

1941 May Day celebration photograph taken outside number 46. The number of children was more than doubled by the presence of the London evacuees who were staying with families in Warkton and Weekley. The May King and Queen this year were Alan Toseland and Rosalind Bagshaw.

May Day celebrations in 1945 the May King was Raymond Bird and his Queen was Muriel Nixon.

Until 1944, the village custom was for the children to carry garlands, form a parade and then proceed to walk the one and a half miles across the pathways to Boughton House where May songs were sung to the Duke and his family. From there they walked around Weekley village singing, and then returned to Warkton for lunch. In the afternoon they once again processed and sung around Warkton village and then about a mile on to Warkton Lodge, returning to the school room for tea prepared by the childrens' mothers.

In 1944 it was decided to confine the celebrations within the village itself.

These festivities comprised a concert performed by the children, who together with the May King and Queen sang and danced to an audience of their families, and friends, as well as The Duke and Duchess on some occasions. Each year the King and Queen were formally crowned by a local dignitary to add excitement to the festivities.

May Day 1948 showing Brenda Toseland being crowned May Queen by Mrs Alice Lamb in the School room. Her consort was Brian Toseland, seen peeping out from behind Mrs Lamb. The festivities were held in the school room on this occasion as it was a very wet day.

May Day 1954 when Jennifer Law at the age of nine was the May Queen. It was not the practice to have a May King at this time.

This photograph shows the last year of the May Day celebrations in Warkton with the children outside the Church in 1956.

King George V Jubilee 1935 The village celebrated by a sports day with afternoon teas, and the planting of two flowering cherry trees on the grass verge outside the large detached cottage, number 19. The trees were planted by Mr Blake & Mr Taffs watched by Mr Charles Lamb and school children. These trees grew on this site for sixty years.

The coronation of King George VI 1937.
This shows Mr Gillings planting the chestnut tree on the village green with the whole village looking on. This chestnut tree is still standing.

Fancy dress competitors celebrating the Coronation of King George VI 1937
Left to right – Helen Toseland, Annie Bagshaw, Jessie Toseland and
Freda Toseland.

204

Fancy dress at a fete in 1943 in aid of war funds. Left to right – Ralph Mutton, Alan Toseland and Mary Page.

School children dancing round the maypole on the Rectory lawn at a village fete in July 1945.

This shows a figure being paraded around the fete, where for twopence, a flag could be purchased and stuck in the body to identify the area of her pain.

WARKTON

CHURCH FETE
AND
FLOWER SHOW

will be held on

SATURDAY, JULY 23rd, 1949.

Opening at 3 p.m.

SALE OF PRODUCE
Following Prize Giving.

Judges : Flowers, Fruit and Vegetables
Mr. E. PALMER and Mr. A. NEAL.

Cakes and Eggs
Mrs. KIDNER and Mrs. SAUNDERS.

Admission : Adults 6d. Children 3d.

Schedules can be obtained from and Entries sent to C. MOIR, 41 Warkton.

ALL CLASSES OPEN.

First Prize 3/-   Second 2/-   Third 1/-   in each class.

DIVISION A.   FLOWERS.

Class
1. Roses, six blooms
2. One Bowl Sweet Peas, with own foliage
3. One Vase Mixed Flowers
4. One Vase Annuals
5. One Fern
6. One Flowering Plant
7. Asters, six

DIVISION B.   VEGETABLES.

Class
8. Potatoes, Dish of six white kidney
9. Potatoes, Dish of six coloured round
10. Peas, twelve pods
11. Runner Beans, twelve
12. Broad Beans, twelve
13. Beetroot, three round
14. Onions, six, shown as grown
15. Carrots, three long
16. Carrots, three short horn
17. Parsnips, three
18. Marrow, one Vegetable
19. Lettuce, two cabbage
20. Cabbage, two
21. Cauliflowers, two
22. Cabbage, two red
23. Cucumber, two ridge, grown outdoors

DIVISION C.   FRUIT.

Class
24. Apples, six cooking
25. Apples, six dessert
26. Gooseberries, twelve
27. One Plate Currants, any variety
28. One Dish Soft Fruit
29. Plums, six

DIVISION D.   SUNDRIES.

Class
30. Plain Cake, approximate weight 2-lb
31. Victoria Sandwich
32. Fruit Cake, approximate weight 2-lb.
33. Hen's Eggs, six, white or brown

RECIPES.   FRUIT CAKE.

4 oz. Margarine, 4 oz. Sugar; 8 oz. Plain Flour, 4 oz. Fruit; Pinch Salt; Baking Powder; 2 Eggs; about 3 tablespoonful Milk. Size of Tin approx. 6 in. diameter and 3 in. deep

PLAIN CAKE.

4 oz. Margarine, 4 oz. Sugar; 8 oz. Self-Raising Flour, 2 Eggs; about ½ a pint Milk, Pinch Salt. Size of Tin approx. 6 in. diameter and 3 in. deep.

VICTORIA SANDWICH.

4 oz. Sugar; 3 Eggs; 4 oz. Margarine; 5 oz. Flour; about 1 tablespoonful Milk, 1 teaspoonful Baking Powder, Pinch Salt.

The annual Church Fete in 1949. This was considered by many to be one of the highlights of the village year.

LADY MARGARET OPENS WARKTON FETE

Lady Margaret Hawkins opened Warkton fete on Saturday. Behind her are Mr. and Mrs. C. Lamb, in the grounds of whose house the fete was held.

DANCING ON THE LAWN AT WARKTON

The grounds of the Old Rectory, Warkton, home of Mr. and Mrs. C. E. Lamb, made a charming setting for a garden fete in aid of Warkton Church, on Saturday.

The fete was opened by Lady Margaret Hawkins, of Grafton Underwood, to whom a bouquet was presented by Marie Kelly.

Truda Ward presented savings envelopes, which represented individual contributions by the villagers, and Roger Porter made a presentation of carnations to Mrs. Lamb.

The fete included a flower, fruit, vegetable and cookery show and reflected the hard work put in by the residents to raise funds for a new heating apparatus for the church.

There were numerous stalls, games and competitions, including archery, clock golf and skittles, for which a pig was presented by the Duke of Buccleuch.

An amusing play, "The Man About the Place," was presented in the garden by Weekley and Warkton Amateur Dramatic Society, produced by Miss Edith Palmer, and the fete concluded with dancing on the lawn.

The opening ceremony of the Church Fete

The bran tub at the Church Fete in 1950.

Children dancing on the Rectory lawn in 1952. A fete was held every year in the village where funds were raised for a variety of charities and appeals. This custom continued until the early 1960s when the school closed and subsequently a committee was formed to use the school as a village hall.

Pipes and Drums Greet the Countess

FETE OPENER

THE skirl of bagpipes welcomed the Earl and Countess of Dalkeith to Warkton on Saturday. Lady Dalkeith went to open the village fete in the grounds of the Old Rectory, home of Mr. C. E. Lamb, and was greeted by the pipes and drums of the Balmoral Girls Pipe Band of Kettering.

It was Lady Dalkeith's first public appearance at Warkton. Introduced by Mr. Lamb, she appealed to her audience to give as generously as they could to the fete in aid of repairs to the village church.

After the opening, the Countess was presented with a bouquet of roses by Elizabeth Dalziel. Mrs. Lamb received a bunch of sweet peas from Caroline Morris.

Lady Dalkeith was dressed in a black costume with cuffed threequarter sleeves and knife pleated skirt, a close-fitting emerald-green hat with matching three quarter gloves and black suede court shoes. She wore a triple string of pearls.

SLOW MARCH

After she had judged the fancy dress competition and presented the prizes, with the Earl and Sir David Scott, she watched the seven pipers and seven drummers perform a slow march on the lawn led by their drum major, Rosalinde Bagshaw, who is a Warkton girl. Later the band formed a ring in which three young girls did Highland dances.

Among those present at the fete were the Rev. C. R. Norcock, vicar of Weekley and Warkton, Mr. J. L. M. Sinnett, agent for the Duke of Buccleuch, and Mrs. Sinnett, and Miss Rhoda Lamb.

RESULTS

Fancy dress, decorated prams, 1 Susan Tyler, 2 Patsy Fleckney. Up to eight years old, 1 Isabel Turner, 2 Sally Eyles, 3 Rodney Rogers, 4 Judith Hubbard. Eight years to 15 years old, 1 Hilary Knight, 2 Brenda Toseland, 3 Susan Chamberlain. Baby show, three months to one

The Countess of Dalkeith presents young Rod Rogers, as a Herald, with his prize, won in the fancy dress contest at Warkton fete on Saturday.

The Countess of Dalkeith presents a prize at the fete in July 1953

Queen Elizabeth II coronation June 3rd 1953 Brian Toseland and Mr Blake planting a Hawthorn tree to mark the occasion. This was on the grass verge opposite the church.

Village sports Coronation Day June 1953
The sports were held between the showers in the road at the bottom of six row as the Playcroft was water logged.

June 3rd 1953
The village school room set out ready for the village Coronation tea. All the village was invited and most attended, where they enjoyed a splendid meal and jolly company.

A village hall Jumble Sale 1960. Since 1869 Jumble Sales were frequently held in the school room in order to raise funds for numerous good causes and charities. Ranging from Kettering Hospital funds to overseas aid. In 1960 four were held and the proceeds went to:

Two went in aid of the church realising £80.2s 6d

One for the Womens' Institute and realised £25

One for the Christmas party for the children from the two villages that realised £22.

This photograph shows part of the outstanding wooden beamed roof structure that is currently hidden by a false ceiling.

The Warkton and Weekley Village Choir in 1934.

The photograph is taken outside the school in Warkton. This choir was flourishing at this time and entered competions that were held as far afield as Oundle and Northampton. In 1934 they won a shield, and in 1936 they won The Cup - the first prize for Village choirs. After these results a social evening was held to celebrate the occasion and this is how the Local Evening Telegraph reported the event.

WARKTON.

SOCIAL EVENING.—An enjoyable evening was spent in the schoolroom on Friday evening by the members and friends of the Weekley and Warkton Choral Society. to celebrate the winning of a cup and shield at the Central Northants Musical Comp, tion, recently held in Northampton. An excellent tea was served to the members by a committee, at which the Rector (the Rev. C. H. L. Hopper) proposed the toast of the Society and conductor, Miss F. M. Lamb, L.R.A.M. After tea friends were invited to the social, an enjoyable evening being spent in community singing, games and dancing.

Lady Burghley presenting the challenge cup given by the late Lord Revelstoke to the conductor of Weekley and Warkton choir at Northamptonshire Musical Festival. On the left is Earl Spencer (president).

This photograph shows Lady Burghley presenting the cup to Miss Florence Lamb of Warkton. On the left of this picture is Earl Spencer of Althorp.

May 1938. Representatives from Warkton who sung in a choir at The Royal Albert Hall in London, at a concert given to commemorate the Coronation of King George VI and Queen Elizabeth. Arthur Toseland, Archie Toseland, Vera Law and Edna Mutton who wore Freda Toseland's wedding dress for the occasion.

Warkton and Weekley Amateur Dramatic Society 1948. The programme shows the cast and production details for 1948

This society was a popular past time for villagers and their productions were well attended and enjoyed by all.

From left to right, Margaret Dalziel, Alec Bagshaw, Eric Sargeant, Mary Turner. This society was active from 1947 until the mid 1950s.

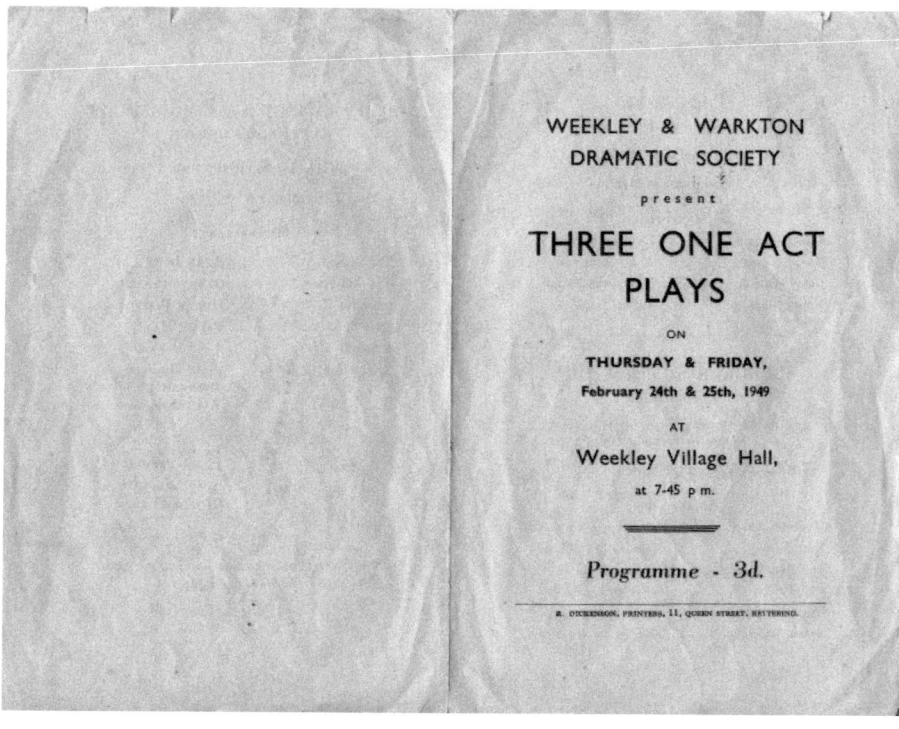

WEEKLEY & WARKTON
DRAMATIC SOCIETY

present

THREE ONE ACT PLAYS

ON

THURSDAY & FRIDAY,

February 24th & 25th, 1949

AT

Weekley Village Hall,

at 7-45 p.m.

Programme - 3d.

R. DICKENSON, PRINTERS, 11, QUEEN STREET, KETTERING.

Eldorado.

by Bernard Gilbert.

SCENE : The Bottom floor of a dis-used Mill.

TIME : A fine morning in March.

CHARACTERS :

James Watson	...	ERIC SARGEANT
Harry Watson	...	ALEC BAGSHAW
Betsy Watson	...	MARGARET DALZIEL
Emma Burrows	...	ELSIE TURNER

Members of the Jury.

by Stuart Ready.

SCENE : The Sitting Room of Margaret Akers house in a small country town.

TIME : Evening in late summer.

CHARACTERS :

Margaret Akers	...	FLORENCE ROWLATT
Mary	...	ROSALIND BAGSHAW
The Hon Mrs. Meadows	...	PAULINE LANE
Miss Prince	...	GWEN WALKER
Paula Stebbings	...	PADDY HAY
Grace Armitage	...	BEATRICE BUSSEY

The Bishop's Candlesticks.

by Norman Mckinnel.

SCENE : The kitchen of the Bishop's Cottage.

TIME : Evening.

CHARACTERS :

The Bishop	...	A. D. LANE
The Convict	...	GEORGE CLARKE
Persomé	...	MIRIAN CLIFFORD
Marie	...	PADDY HAY
Sergeant	...	JOHN SHATFORD
Gendarmes	...	JOHN BIRD
		BERTRAM LUMBERS
		ALAN KIRKMAN

Producer	...	EDITH PALMER
Stage Managers	...	ALEC BAGSHAW
		GEORGE CLARKE

The Society wishes to thank all who have given their help and support.

The Village Club, was provided by the Estate, for the men of the village and Estate workers in the old blacksmith's stables, in the centre of the village, and was managed on a non profit making basis. The Club was a male only environment until the early 1960s, when women were admitted. In the late 1960s it closed completely.

This photograph shows club members enjoying a game of Whist.

The interior of the Village Club in 1950, on the occasion of the annual dinner. Men used to enjoy games of skittles, darts, dominoes and cards, whilst drinking their pints of beer.

Club members in 1950. from left to right, Albert Law, Ken Crawley, Tim Issitt, Douglas Furnell.

Notice the stove in the foreground, this was used for heating the club and a similar one was in use at the school. On both premises when the wind was in the wrong direction, it filled the building with smoke and any persons inside had to vacate the site until it cleared, sometimes over three or four hours. From the school's point of view the children loved this as it meant missing lessons. At the club the chimney from this stove came out fairly low down on the wall. There was a regular habit on November 5th, that mischievous lads would climb up to this chimney and drop fireworks down the stove pipe. All hell was let loose with the men rushing out to try to catch the culprits but they were too fast to be caught. Eventually the men got wise to this and one year, hid in the yard, when the boys duly arrived armed with ammunition the men caught them and gave them a clip round the ear. The boys got their own back as on the next night they climbed up and stuffed a sack down the chimney thus smoking the men out. After this episode things quietened down and on future years the men were left in peace.

Warkton Victoria Football team 1900. This team played against other local village teams.

Warkton and Weekley Cricket team in 1903. The team played on a pitch to the left of the church behind the Vicarage at Weekley. They played in the local village league.

After the First World War the team moved to their present pitch which is situated just inside Boughton Park adjacent to the church.

The Cricket Team in 1950.

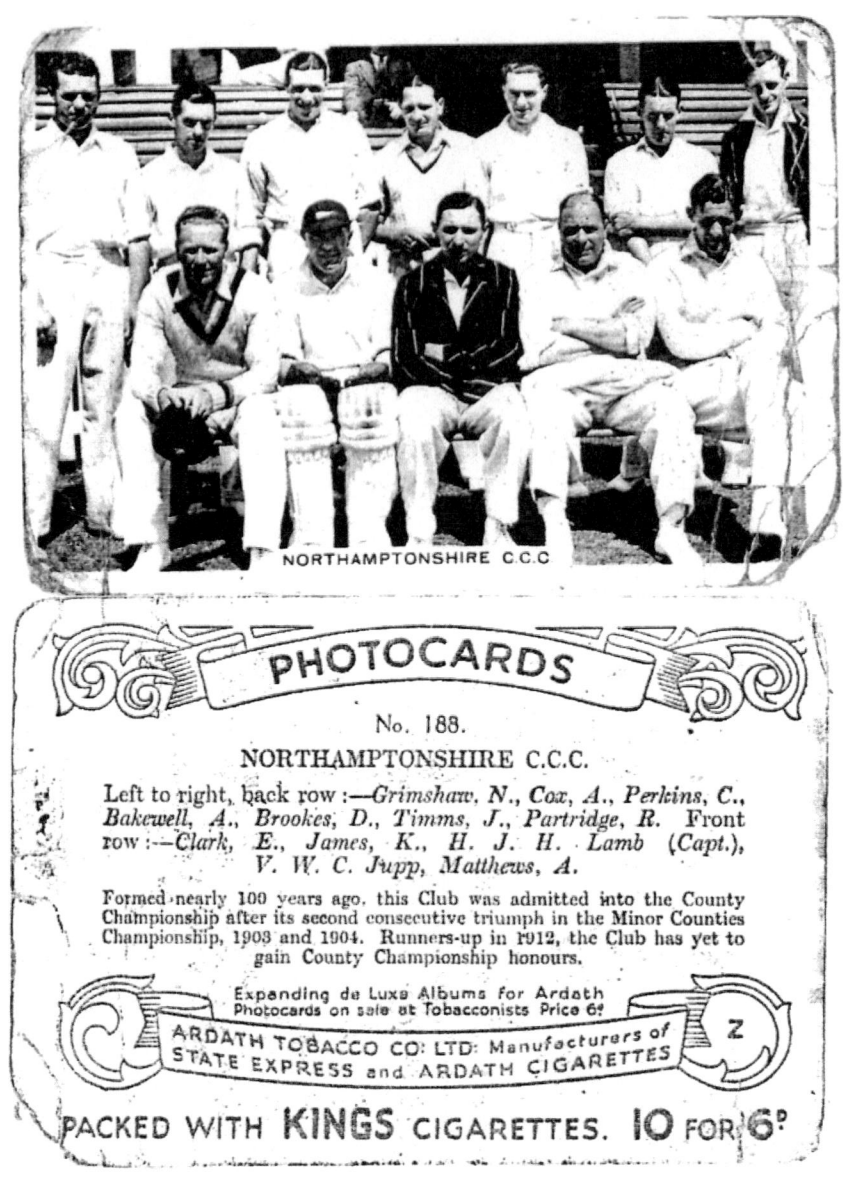

Henry John Hey Lamb played 38 matches for Northamptonshire County Cricket Club and captained the County side. He was a forceful batsman who also kept wicket. He had a long connection with Kettering Town Cricket Club, serving as Captain, Chairman and then as President for 27 years, and was even featured on a cigarette card as illustrated.

Dorothy Margaret (Margot) Lamb. She was a keen sportswomen and played for Kettering Ladies Hockey Club. Margot is on the extreme left of the back row.

This week's picture from the past features Kettering Ladies' Hockey Club, during the 1936-37 season. Pictured left to right are: (back row) Margot Whistler (Mrs H. J. H. Lamb), Diana King (Mrs J. H. Cheaney), Joy Newton (Mrs R. W. Kilsby), Millie Allan (Mrs Holland), Madge Ingram (Mrs Lane deceased), Elsie Aldwinckle. (Seated) Beryl Elmore (Mrs Bandy), Marjorie Hudson (now vice-president), Jessie Robinson (Mrs Harrap), Joan Martin (Mrs Maxdecal), Rene Bryan (Mrs D. J. Martin: now club president).

The Kettering Beekeepers Association met occasionally at Warkton. The picture taken in the late 1940s, shows a meeting held in the rectory grounds, with Florence Lamb seated fourth left from the speaker. Mr Sumpter, a member, used to keep about a dozen hives in the orchard next to the church.

WOODLAND PYTCHLEY AT WARKTON.

Woodland Pytchley Hunt at their annual meeting at Warkton 1930, watched by numerous hunt followers and spectators.

The Hunt and followers leaving the Village in 1936. At this time they did not have to worry about too much traffic on the roads, unlike today.

The Woodland Pytchley Hunt meet March 1961 on the village green.

Alec Bagshaw and Arthur Toseland with their motor cycles in 1932. Motor cycles were becoming increasingly popular due to the high price of motor cars.

Alec Bagshaw's Car in 1933

Cyril Toseland's Humber car in 1934

Mr and Mrs Dalziel preparing to leave for Buckingham Palace, where she was to receive the B.E.M. awarded for her dedication to The National Savings Association.

Christmas Dinner in the Village Hall C1980. From left to right, Hilda Owen, John Lamb, Amy Gudyer. Until the school closed in 1961, Christmas Dinner was provided annually for the children. The school premises were

subsequently used as the Village Hall. A committee was formed to run activities for the village, and Christmas dinner was one of the most popular events.

The Village Hall Committee 2001 serving the Christmas Dinner in the Village Hall.

Christmas Dinner being enjoyed by villagers and friends in 2001. This is currently a biennial popular village event

Occupations

Farming has been an integral part of village life for centuries. From estate records of the early eighteenth century we know that there were eight farms in the village. These would have varied in size and the numbers of villagers employed at different seasons. When the villagers had no work on the farms they would have found work gathering stone and repairing the roads which in the winter times were in an appalling state of repair.

In 1777 according to the Montagu's Muster List, there were 9 farmers in the village. Farmers were able to have the use of the village bull to service their cows, during the 1700s. The Village Overseer had charge of the bull. This was known as Bull Levies, which was a record of the money paid for the use of the bull at 9d per cow, if required a second time 6d and a third at 3d.

For the year 1783 there were 21 farmers/smallholders who paid levies for a total of 108 cows, realising a figure of £4 1s 0d. In 1791 fourteen farmers/smallholders used the bull's services.

In 1788 George Cave, Overseer bought a bull at Whitsun Fair for £4 9s 0d. and he was paid 1s 0d for buying the bull.

Warkton Overseer's record of the Bull dated 1790.

In 1900 there were a number of smallholdings and three farms.

Ise Farm was farmed by Arthur Turner, apart from the small field around the house, he had the field immediately after the Lime Avenue, on the left of the Grafton Road. This was the old Warkton Allotment field, called Thimble Green. He also had two fields behind this towards the Wilderness, Moorfield and Jacobs Hedge and on the right hand side of the road a field called Strennage 1. The next field was also called Strennage but at that time the Turner's did not farm it, they acquired that with other fields at a later date. These are now in the hands of Boughton Estates.

The Elms (now known as Fedwells Farm) was farmed by Mrs Wells on her own after the death of her husband, in 1880. This farm has changed hands a number of times during the last 150 years. Mr Melkins, then Mr and Mrs Wells, and Robert Brett followed by George Hay, Peter Hay, John Bird and currently the Steeples family.

Jack Mutton who was employed by Mr Brett was a notorious poacher. He had a percussion cap muzzle loading gun, with the hammer broken off. He carried a pebble in his pocket and to fire the gun he tapped the cap with it. He very rarely missed his quarry, and he kept the gun hidden under a manger at New Lodge Farm. The Elms was one of the larger farms in the village. Apart from several fields around the house it comprised all the fields from the farmhouse along the bridle path, through the spinney at Barton Seagrave, including The New Lodge, (now demolished) which is most of the land where the Ise Village is located.

The Ise Village was built during the 1960s/1970s to accommodate the need for additional family homes in the borough, resulting in Kettering becoming much closer to Warkton.

The Firs, named because it had two large fir trees at the front of the house, was farmed by Henry Knight. Prior to this, when the Panthers occupied the farmhouse, it was known as Manor House Farm. After Henry Knight came Charles Dunkley and then Hedley Lomas. This was the largest farm in Warkton, together with the fields around the farmhouse, it also included the pasture fields on the Kettering side of the brook, along the now Deeble Road. It also had a lot of arable land along Warkton Lane. This farm has now been taken in hand by Boughton Estates.

The smallholdings within the parish in 1900 were:

Number 19, occupied by Mr Wells, who was a relative of the Wells family at the Elms.

Number 31, when the pub closed in 1874, it became a smallholding, and was run by Mr Clifford, followed by Ted Mutton, who later moved into number 44. Jimmy Sargeant, followed by his son Eric, took over number 31 in the 1930's until Eric retired. This smallholding had the first field up the hill on the right leaving Warkton called Pond Close and the Playcroft next to the school, the Lime Avenue fields both sides of the road and the field called Overwort.

Number 44 was a smallholding run by Bill Taylor who also worked on the Estate.

Number 45 this was a smallholding worked by three brothers named Fletcher, who were gamekeepers on the Estate. It was subsequently run by Mr Rush from 1913 until 1933 when it ceased to be a smallholding and Mr George Toseland occupied the house.

Number 46 was a smallholding until the latter part of the 18th century. Mr Bagshaw from Grafton Underwood farmed there, moving from Grafton in 1830. He was also the butcher and had a shop built on to the end of the house.

Number 7 The Gables was also a smallholding. Run by Mr Fred Mutton. Their milking shed was to the right of the house.

Tree Nurseries in Warkton

There were three known Tree Nurseries planted with different varieties of willows, mainly grown for domestic use, some being sold for making cricket bats. The earliest one was behind houses number 5 and 6 and was closed in the 1880's. One was in the field on the left behind the now demolished threshing barn. The poor people of the village were able to take their corn, which after enclosure, was gleaned from the fields after the crop had been harvested, to be threshed in the barn, using a hand flail. This practice ceased at the close of the nineteenth century. The third nursery was on the left of the gravel path leading to Boughton House.

Some of these trees are still standing although no longer worked, coppiced every second year which ceased in the 1950's.

In what was known as Polly Mutton's field, the field to the south of the church there were five large walnut trees, 2 adjacent to the church wall, two at the road side and one further along the field. These were felled in 1930.

Village Allotments

Almost every household in Warkton had an allotment in the 1800's which was given to them to compensate for the loss of their common rights at enclosure in 1810.

These allotments were at first in the field called Thimble Green on the left past the Lime Avenue on the Grafton Road. For some reason in the latter part of the 19th century these were moved to Long Leas, the field on the right just before the turn into Warkton Lane. There were about 35 plots but by the mid 1960s there were no allotments in use in the village.

Warkton with Little Oakley were two of the last villages in the county to be enclosed in 1810. Enclosure caused great distress to the people who had common rights, as they lost the privilege of grazing their animals on the common. Not all people could have access to the common only farmers, people who owned their own homes and ancient cottagers. In Warkton's case no one owned their own house other than the Rector. They were all owned by the Duke of Buccleuch. The common was a considerable distance from the village in the north of the parish, and is still known as Warkton Common to this day, and is mostly woodland.

Geo Cave a Count of the Turnups

Pd for Cutting of faggots	1	14 4
Pd for too Ringes of wood	1	13 4
Pd for Rending the Stakes	0	2 0
Pd for faggotting the Ringes	0	6 3
Pd for hogen the turnups hog	1	10 10
Gave them to Drink	0	1 6
Pd for Loading the faggots	0	9 2
Gave him to Drink	0	0 2
Pd Brancon of Goddinton for Stakes	2	10 0
Spent	0	0 6
Pd Ed Brampton for Stakes	0	9 6
Pd Robt Cave for Ditto	0	10 0
Pd Jos meadows for Dito	0	5 0
my Self for Dito	1	7 6
Pd John Green for Dito	1	1 10
Pd for the Seed ninty pounds	1	2 6
Pd for Cyzeing the Turnups		
Gave them to Drink	0	2 0
for Riteing up the Loos thams after the hogos	0	0 6
for Righteing the Leavi	0	1 0
Total Expence	£ 16	11
The Leavie Collects	16	8 11
Due to the town	£ 0	8 0
Due to the town		

George Cave Overseer's count of the turnips for 1787. This shows a list of tasks performed and monies paid for the aforesaid. It was an annual account compiled by the Overseer relating to the government directive stating that turnips and relevant crops must be grown in every community, in order to promote self sustainability in the event of famine or other disasters. In this year there were nineteen individuals who were obliged to grow turnips etc.

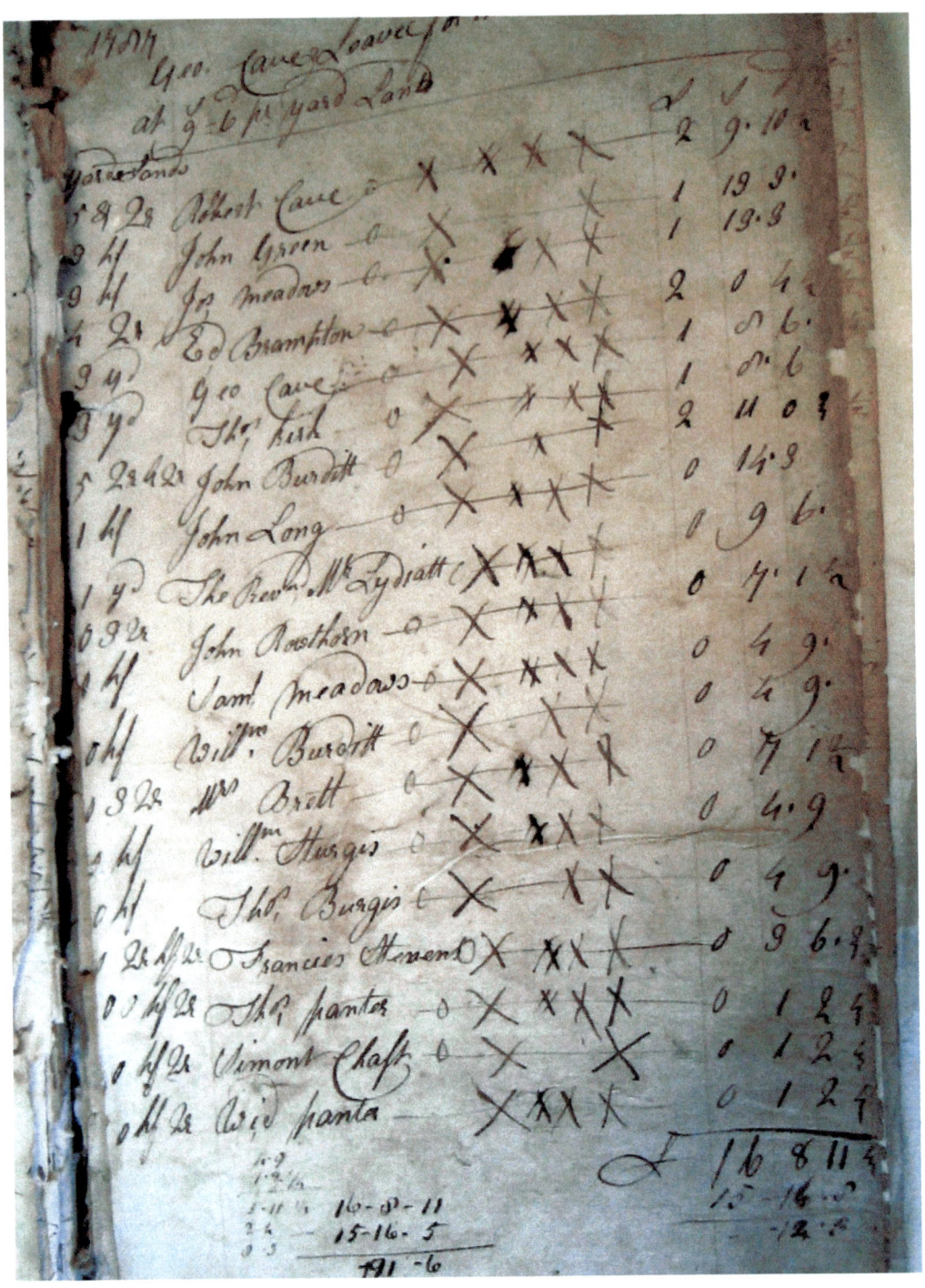

Showing yardlands held and rent paid by the farmers of Warkton for growing turnips in 1787.

C1895 A group of farm labourers taking a lunch break while harvesting oats and tares (using scythes) in a field adjacent to Warkton Lane, on Henry Knight's farm.

A Warkton farm labourer mowing wheat with a scythe as late as 1939. This would be corn flattened by a storm, and hand mowed as the binder could not harvest such damaged crops.

A group of men in1898, mowing wheat with a horse drawn binder, in a field off the Grafton road, showing the lime tree avenue in the background.

The second man from the left, Mr Cave, would for a wager carry a hundred weight sack of corn from Warkton to Kettering without once setting it down. Charles Law, aged 33, on the binder, and the man on the extreme left William Law, aged 77, were tragically struck with typhoid fever soon after this picture was taken and died on the same day. In the Warkton parish registers it states that never in the annals of Warkton parish have two men been buried in the evening immediately after their death. Unfortunately William's wife who was Charles's mother, caught the same fever and died two days later. The lad on the lead horse, Harry Taylor, lived at number 18 all his life and he died in 1981 aged 92.

Note the horse drawn operations of a binder. It was a heavy machine, that often required three horses to pull it, the mechanism was driven from the large wheel under the appliance.

Depending on the size of the field, or how much of corn had been cut, the horses were changed on alternate rounds of the standing corn. There was one horse either side of the draw pole and one in front called the lead horse which had a rider to steer it. This was usually a boy. On the binder itself, controlling the machinery sat a driver.

Two men mowing wheat at Warkton C1910. This photograph shows three draw horses behind the lead horse, one must assume that this was on heavy land.

Agricultural workers threshing corn in 1932 at the New Lodge Warkton.

FIVE STACKS BURNT OUT IN FIERCE WARKTON BLAZE.

A fire at New Lodge Farm in October 1934. The fire chief thought that this fierce blaze would spread to the house and thus instructed the family to remove their possessions with help from the surrounding villagers. In the event the house was saved.

Harvesting oats on the Toseland's farm Warkton in 1950. A tractor and binder was being used, showing Cyril Toseland, in the centre, with a gun that he used to shoot rabbits as they were disturbed in the field. As the area of standing corn got smaller, to about an acre, the binder would stop and beaters, who were mainly boys, would walk through the remaining corn, to flush out the rabbits which were than shot by men with shot guns. These rabbits were a welcome addition to the family's diet, and were used in stews and pies. Surplus rabbits were given to other villagers for their supper.

Carrying the harvested crop from the field to the farm, where it would have been stacked to await the arrival of the threshing machine. These machines were contracted to farms where they would thresh the crop. (Threshing machines separated the corn from the chaff and straw. This operation required at least eight men to fulfil all the tasks. Women and young boys were employed in the dirtiest and dusty job which involved cleaning out the chaff and cavings from under the drum. The corn was bagged up, and taken to the corn merchants. The chaff was a by-product that was commonly used for animal husbandry. The straw was either baled or stacked loose to be used for animal feed and bedding throughout the winter.) A popular pastime that took place whilst threshing, was that young boys with dogs would wait around to catch the rats as they ran out when the stack got smaller.

It was compulsory during the war years to put wire netting round the stack before work commenced, to catch as many rats as possible. Although quite a number would get over the wire if one was not quick enough. On one occasion whilst threshing a stack of wheat, 84 rats were caught and left in a heap overnight. On returning in the morning it was discovered that all theses rats were gone, taken by owls or foxes.

Threshing and baling straight from the field on Turners farm in 1950. This was only done if either the corn was required for the next seasons seed or the straw was needed for immediate use.

1956 A Combine Harvester in Warkton. This was a period when combines became more common and the traditional methods became obsolete. The first combines were known as "baggers" where the threshed corn was deposited in sacks, unlike today when the corn is conveyed back to the farm loose.

Archie Toseland baling the straw from the combine using a pick up baler in 1956.

Haymaking C1900 in Warkton. The crop was brought from the field and stored, using an elevator to get the hay from the cart into the barn. The horse on the right is working the machinery, by walking around in a circular motion, that in turn drives the elevator. The trap door in the roof was finally removed in 2003.

Haymaking in 1900, in this photograph, the horse turning the machinery is on the left and the horse on the right has just brought a load of hay from the field, with the men ready to unload the hay onto the elevator.

Ted Fleckney and Syd Nixon haymaking in 1948 using a horse drag, to gather the hay which was then made into haycocks. These stood in the field for approximately one week and the hay was then carted back loose to the farm, to be stacked until required for animal feed in the winter months.

Farm workers loading hay onto an elevator in 1937 at New Lodge Farm Warkton. This machine is being driven by a small Lister petrol engine.

Haymaking in 1933. Showing the ladies having a picnic in the field with the farmers. This practice of bringing a picnic to the farmers in the field saved valuable daylight hours during the hay time and harvest season.

Cyril Toseland baling hay in 1952. This method made the transportation of hay much easier and quicker for the farmer, and reduced the amount of labour required.

Schoolgirls from Northampton and Broughton are working as potato pickers on the Glebe Farm of Mr. Ernest Palmer, nurseryman, of Warkton Lodge, Warkton. Kettering children can only go on the farms after school hours, unofficially. Mr. Palmer is continually faced with the difficulty of small change, because the children like to be paid individually, and not collectively in groups.

School children potato picking at Warkton Lodge farm in 1942. They were paid 2s 6d per day. Although back breaking work it was a good excuse to miss school for a few days and an opportunity to earn some pocket money.

Ted Nixon, with "Blossom" carting manure to be spread on the fields as a fertiliser in 1948. The manure had to be loaded into the cart with a muck fork, and then spread over the fields using the same fork.

One of George Toseland's horses, Bonny, in 1939.

Pat Ball and Alan Toseland with Bess in 1951

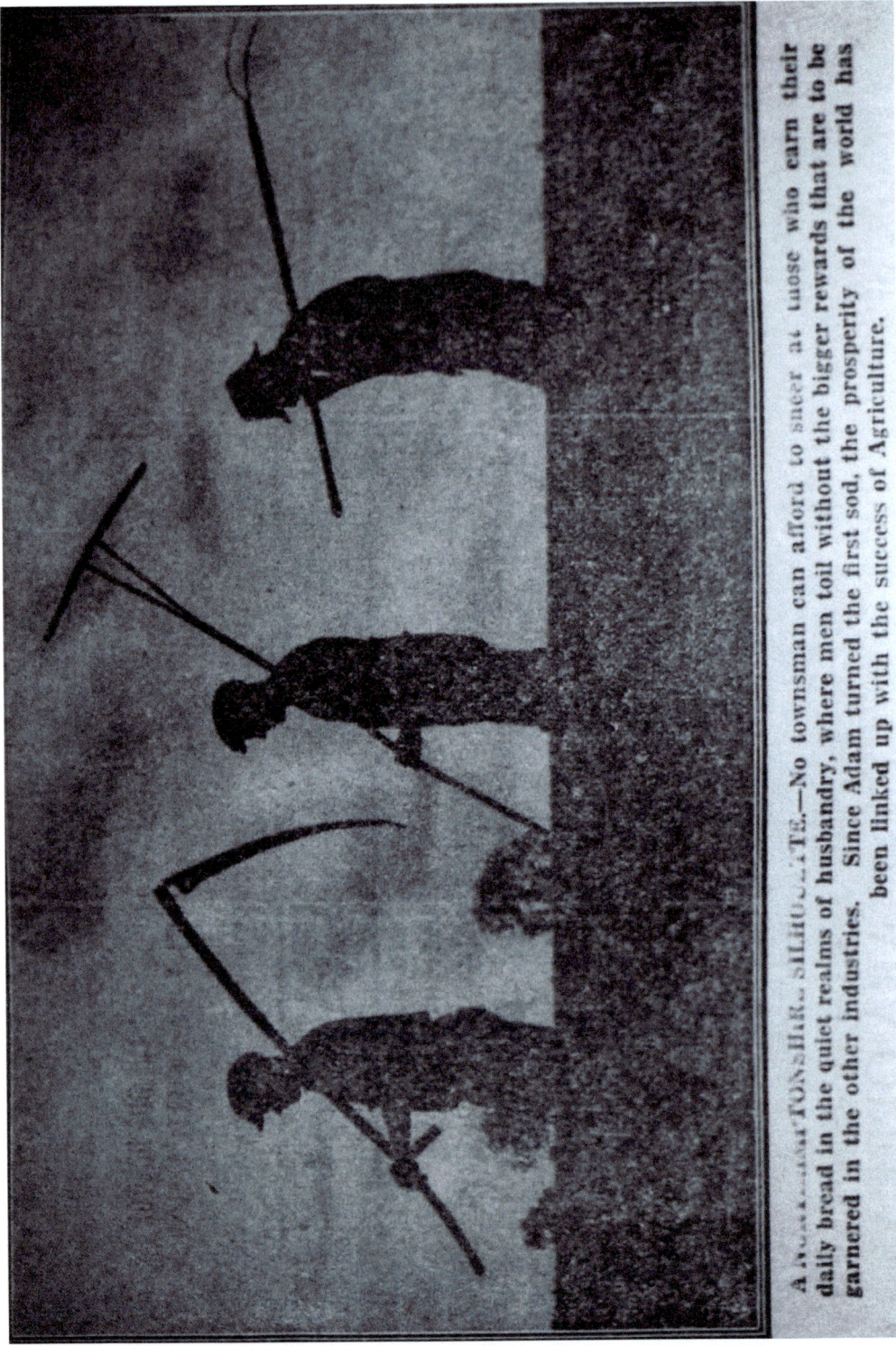

A ————— ——— ——————.—No townsman can afford to sneer at those who earn their daily bread in the quiet realms of husbandry, where men toil without the bigger rewards that are to be garnered in the other industries. Since Adam turned the first sod, the prosperity of the world has been linked up with the success of Agriculture.

1932 June. Farm labourers returning home after a days toil in the fields, showing the tools of the trade, a scythe, a rake and a pitchfork.

Bob Nixon at the Northants County Show in September 1965. He worked for Hedley Lomas at Moorfield Farm who had a large herd of over 150 Friesian Cows.

Keith Arthey with a Charolais calf in 1965. This was the first Charolais calf to be born in the County. Keith had thirty five milking cows and approximately thirty five acres of mixed arable and grassland at Warkton Lodge Farm which is located off Warkton Lane. He was a member of Kettering Rural District Council and retired to Little Oakley.

Charlie Lewis who worked for Peter Hay at Fedwells Farm with a new Ford tractor outside the rear of his house, number 34, in 1965.

The Wars

The first known armed conflict that involved Warkton, was in the year 1065, when Northamptonshire was attacked and defeated by an army from Northumberland led by Morcar.

Nothing more is known about any further military forays until 1605 when a militia was formed all over England to repel any seaborne invasions. The muster roles for all towns and villages in East Northants were held at Boughton House. In these roles from 1605 to approximately1650, Warktons' entry was:

1 corslett held by the Rev Stone.

1 trayned man a Thomas Croft

there were no light horses or caribinors

This entry remained the same, with the exception of the 1630 entry that included 2 trayned men. (a corselet was defensive cover for the body made chiefly from leather).

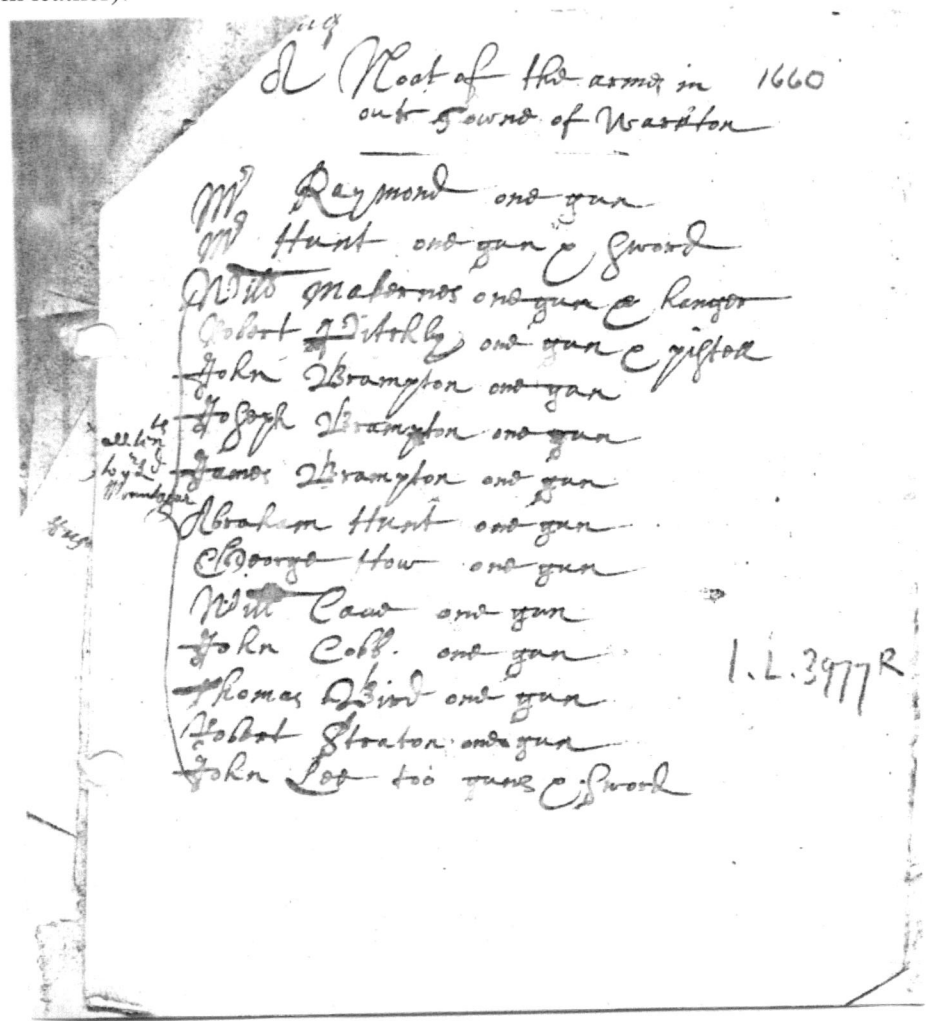

1660 account of the arms held in Warkton.

After 1650 all eligible males had to be listed for liable military service.

252

A List of the Names that are liable
To serve in the Militia   Warkton

Immanuel Mutton Farmer
John Humphrey Farmer
John Craft Labourer
Thomas Meadows Weaver
William Marshall Farmer
Thomas Pain Labourer
John Bean Labourer
John Caves Farmer
John Cox Rector Man
William Burdill Farmer
Joseph March Labourer
Joseph Night Weaver
John Hunter Weaver Lame
Andrew Weding Farmer
William Dains Farmer
Sollomon Panter Cordwinder
William Sturges Farmer
Thomas Goode Labourer
Thomas Burges Joyner
John Ward Miller
Samuel Smith Farmer   Lame
James Cockin Farmer
Frances Bibby Farmer Lame
Thos Cox Farmer
John Compton Farmer
John Chapman Game Keeper
Frances Stevens Carpender   23
James New Weaver   infirm

If any thinks Themselves aggrieved the
Must appeal to the White Hart in Kettering
On Thursday next John Green Constable

1781
List of
eligible
males in
Warkton.

253

This militia requirement lasted for nearly 200 years. Through the English Civil war which began in 1642, there is no record of any action nearer than Naseby. Although Boughton was a Royalist encampment there is no record of a direct attack on the Estate. The only mention of the Civil war is in the Warkton burial records which states that on 11th June 1645 a soldier killed Edward Holm, whose body lies in the churchyard.

However, the Rector of Warkton at the time of the Civil war Nickolas Eastwick stated in 1643, " *even in this somewhat remote place the effect of the war were being felt*" In a letter to Edward 1st Lord Montagu, " *he prays that peace may come*" adding *"we do already taste the miseries of civil war"*.

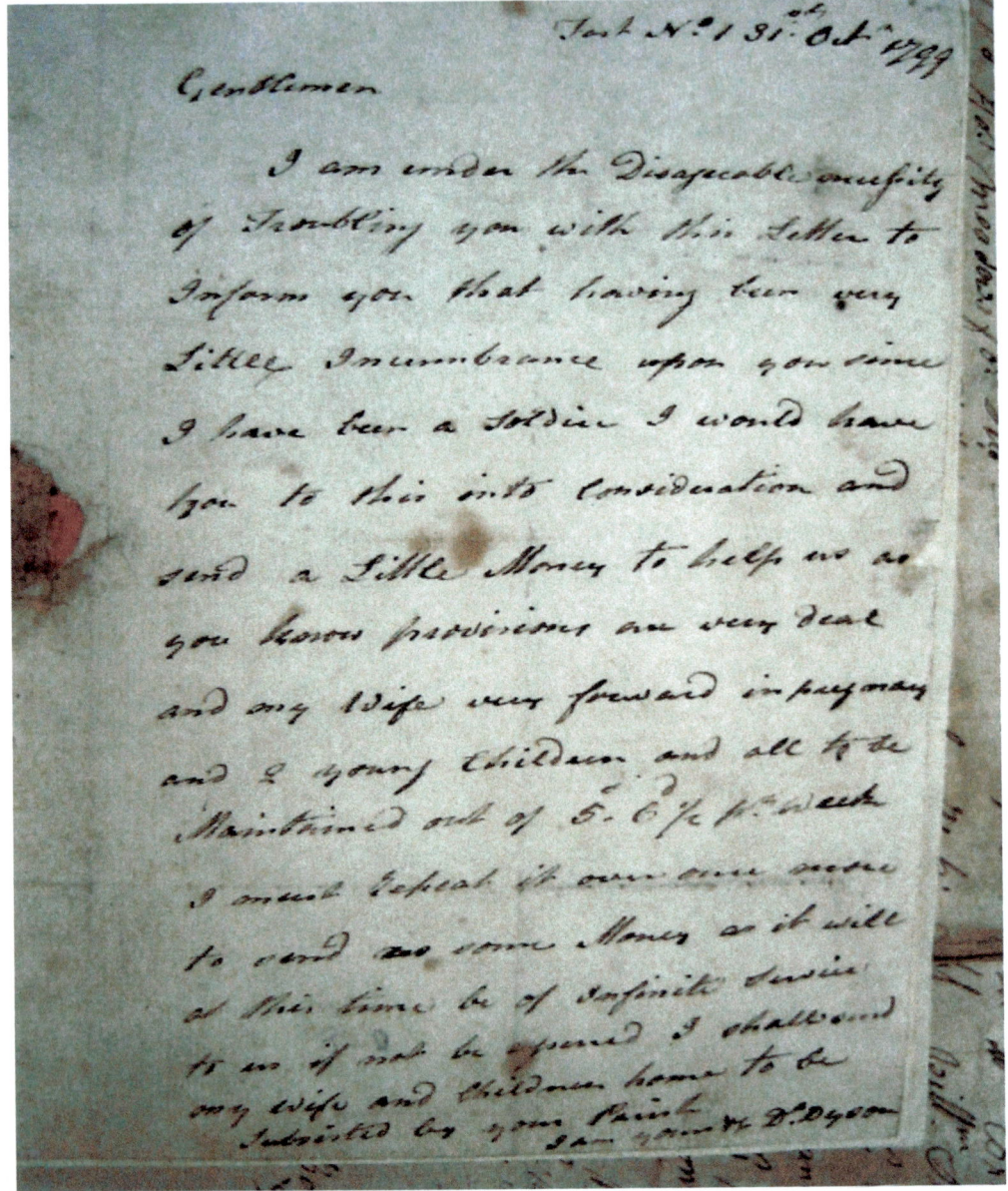

First World War 1914-18

Thirty five Warkton men enlisted into the army, 9 into the Northamptonshire's and the remainder into other regiments with 1 man joining the navy and serving on HMS Terrible.

During the war 6 men were lost in action:

January 1916 Private William Swingler Northamptonshire Regiment, killed on the Somme.

October 1917 Gunner Arthur Bagshaw R.G.A. killed by an enemy shell whilst entering a dugout at Ypres.

October 1917 Private Archibald Sargeant The Buffs East Kent Regiment. He was killed at Ypres after serving only 8 months, and has no known grave.

December 1917 Private Horace Mutton Essex Regiment. Captured in Iraq and died as a prisoner of war in Turkey 2 years to the day of his enlistment. He is buried in Baghdad.

April 1918 Private Eric Bagshaw (Arthur Bagshaws' nephew) Royal West Surrey Regiment, killed in action in Belgium and he has no known grave.

August 1918 Private William Brett Wales Royal Fusiliers. Killed in France after only 3 weeks there.

Only 5 men are commemorated on the war memorial, the 6th, Private Swingler is on Loddington's war memorial as he was working there when he enlisted.

(right)

In 1699 a letter from a Warkton boy, David Dyson, who was called up into active service in the militia, and stationed at Rye in Kent. In the Overseer's accounts for that period there are numerous payments recorded to the Militiaman at 5s 0d per quarter and in at least two cases, David Dyson's name is mentioned. Plus one payment of 8s 6d to send him to Rye barracks in Kent and two weeks later the same amount to send his wife and two children there.

EXTRACT FROM THE EVENING TELEGRAPH 1919
DISTINGUISHED SERVICE

Military Cross Awarded to Captain G. F. Whistler of Warkton

CAPT. G. F. WHISTLER

Last week the King approved of immediate awards for conspicuous gallantry and devotion to duty in North Russia, conferred by Major-General C. C. M. Maynard, C.B., C.M.G., D.S.O., in pursuance of the powers vested in him by His Majesty. Amongst these honours the Military Cross was conferred upon Lieut. (T./Capt.) G. F. Whistler, R.F.A. - At Tulgas, on April 25th, a mutiny occurred among the Russian troops. His prompt action in shooting a mutineer saved the lives of two other officers. He subsequently took charge and carried out the retirement of the guns from Tulgas with great ability. His courage and devotion to duty had the effect of keeping the Russian artillery personnel loyal.

Captain G. F. Whistler's name also appeared amongst the recipients of the King's Birthday Honours, when he was awarded the M.B.E. (Military Division).

Reverend Whistler's eldest son, Godfrey Fuller Whistler, gained The Military Cross and The Order of St Anne of Russia for conspicuous gallantry and devotion to duty in North Russia.

(left)
George Toseland Suffolk
Regiment 1918.
George lived at number 25 and
served in the First World War.
After he was demobbed he
returned to Warkton and worked
on the estate, until he started
farming 106 acres of land at the
old nursery to the rear of number
45, in his own right in 1933.

(below)
Bert Wadsworth (on the left)
a local Warkton boy who
served in the First World War,
and returned safely. This was
taken in France in 1917.

Hay for the Army.

Smart Work by the Women Land Workers.

This photograph taken from the newspaper shows First World War Women Land Workers baling hay for the army. This was in fields just east of the village in July 1918.

April 1918 showing Doris Swingler a milkmaid on a farm in Warkton.

July 1917 a picture of two volunteer milkmaids. There were three Land Army girls attached permanently to Warkton farms in the Great War, they only carried out milkmaid duties.

The Second World War 1939 - 1945

This photograph shows John Lamb in Calcutta, fourth from the right in the middle row. John served in the Royal Corps of Signals from 1940 to 1946, attaining the rank of Lieutenant Colonel. He was stationed at Catterick and then at Bury St Edmunds, being posted in 1943 to the Claims Commission at Salisbury as a Captain. After a few months he was posted to India as a Major. He spent some time in Bombay and in July 1944, was posted to Calcutta as Assistant Director of Claims Southern Command, with the rank of Lieutenant Colonel.

Throughout the war, Warkton's Local Defence Volunteers (LDVs) later to be called the Home Guard, were an active force in the village. With the ever increasing news of enemy advances on the continent, on 14th May 1940, the government appealed on the nine o'clock news, for men between the ages of 17 and 65, and not otherwise engaged in military service to enrol at their local police station to join the LDVs. Sixteen men from Warkton volunteered immediately, with Donovan Lane taking the position of Captain. Training began almost at once, they had lectures in the school room and patrolled the local area every night. There was a lookout post on the top of the water tank at the reservoir on Warkton lane, where incidentally, on the night that Coventry was bombed, and also when London docks took their direct hit, the fires from both these cities could be seen across the sky line.

Warkton was designated to be a closed village i.e. it would be defended in the event of an invasion. There were two road blocks that could be erected at very short notice. One was below the reservoir in Warkton Lane, the other at the bottom of the village where the telephone box is now situated. These consisted of round concrete cylinders, with a hole through the centre, weighing 2-3 cwts, that could be rolled into the road and secured with iron bars let into holes in the road. There were hundreds of sand bags stacked beside the road ready to be placed round these concrete blocks. On one occasion the village lads thought that they would do their bit to help and placed these sand bags across the road, thus effectively obstructing the traffic, until the local Policeman came along who made the lads stack them all back up again with a strict telling off.

There was a slit trench dug behind the hedge opposite number 7, still to be seen today, and another at the side of the road leading towards Grafton. These were to be used as machine gun posts in the event of attack.

Early in 1940, when there was a real threat of invasion a battalion of regular troops appeared in the village and one or two armed men were posted at almost every house with Bren gun carriers hidden under trees and other army vehicles spread about the village. Explosives were placed under the bridge and wired ready for blowing to hold up any potential enemy advance. The Home Guard instructions were to carry on their normal daytime work until an attack was forthcoming, in which case they were to assist the regular army in defending the village.

The church bells were to be rung to signal an invasion. All church bells were silenced at the beginning of the war as ordered by the government, and were only to be rung to signal an emergency. On hearing the bells the men, who mostly carried their rifles at all times, were to cease work and go to their headquarters at the school, to collect their orders. This particular threat diminished after 48 hours and the army was stood down. The first time that church bells were rung in war time was in October 1942 when Churchill requested that they were to be rung to celebrate the victory at El Alamein.

Another serious alert came on 7th September 1940 when the Home Guard were virtually on their own, as most of the regular forces had been sent to defend the coast. Alfred Tosleand, a sergeant in the Home Guard related the following:

"The Home Guard and regular troops were put on "red alert" in response to secret service intelligence reports intimating an imminent German invasion. German paratroopers were expected to land at midnight on 7th September to take all aerodromes, especially in the Midlands. An invasion of England was anticipated as France and the Low Countries had recently fallen. Regular troops were guarding the east coast against seaborne attacks and London was heavily guarded with anti –aircraft guns leaving the Midlands vulnerable to airborne invasion. All farmers were instructed to place their farm implements and other obstacles in the middle of the fields to prevent gliders from landing unharmed. Warkton Home Guard company of just 14 men were instructed to proceed to the partly built aerodrome at

Grafton Underwood, along with the village companies of Brigstock, Geddington and Cranford. Kettering and other village platoons were stationed in Kettering to guard vital areas such as the Police Station, telephone exchange, gas water and electricity services. The village companies were instructed to guard the aerodrome and to take no prisoners, all German paratroopers were to be shot on sight. The Warkton Home Guard company said their farewells, and met at the HQ which was the School. Here they formed up and proceeded to march to Grafton Underwood aerodrome. Each man had a rifle, and the company was armed with Sten guns, a machine gun and grenades, the one thing that they had plenty of was ammunition. Luckily for everyone Hitler postponed the invasion indefinitely. Although there were many scares and incidents, as the weeks and months went by, that night was potentially the most serious and dangerous night of the war for Warkton."

As part of the training for action mock battles were frequently staged between local platoons. At one of these training events, Cranford Home Guard was to be the enemy and had to attack Warkton. At one point a Warkton man pointed his rifle at his opponent and said *"you are dead"* at this stage the opponent disagreed and then the real fighting began, bayonets were drawn and both men had to be restrained by their platoon members.

At another incident Warkton and Grafton Home Guard were acting as German parachutists, armed with apples for grenades. They had to capture three key points in Kettering, the Police Station, the Post Office/Telephone Exchange and the Electricity Company. Kettering and other Home Guard platoons with elements of regular soldiers being the defenders based their strategy upon the defence of the roads. Warkton and Grafton, knowing the local fields well, followed the course of the brook and crept into the town unchallenged. Two platoon members acted as decoys and whilst keeping to the road managed to capture the two Kettering men who were guarding Warkton bridge. The others crossed the fields and reached the police station via back streets, and taking the one guard on the door prisoner, they rushed inside throwing their "apples" at an inspector who was sitting at his desk, telling him he was dead. Meanwhile other men captured their objectives without losing any of their platoon members. So it could be said that Warkton and Grafton won the day.

The nearest Warkton got to any danger was in 1942 when a bomb was dropped in a field between the village and Boughton House. A string of nine bombs had been dropped across the railway lines near to the Kettering furnaces, this was the last of the nine bombs.

The only damage was a large crater in the field, and a herd of frightened cows huddled together in the corner of the field. The Home Guard was called out to investigate.

One event in 1943 involved a crashed aircraft on the Grafton road. This was a Halifax from Leeming Bar in Yorkshire that was returning from a raid and was fatally damaged, on fire and unable to make an emergency landing. The crew had baled out over the coast, leaving just the pilot who lost his life. The Home Guard, that was on duty, went to the scene and mounted guard until regular troops arrived to take charge. Any possible rescue attempts were severely hampered by exploding ammunitions and the possibility of unexploded bombs.

Warkton was declared an open village in November 1943, which meant that in the event of any enemy opposition, they would be able to proceed through the village, with only light harassment until they reached the next defended town or village. There were many incidents, some amusing and some more serious that involved the local Home Guard units, but there are too many to relate here.

Cyril Toseland 1940 a member of Warkton Home Guard.

Certificate of Proficiency

HOME GUARD

On arrival at the Training Establishment, Primary Training Centre or Recruit Training Centre, the holder must produce this Certificate at once for the officer commanding, together with Certificate A if gained in the Junior Training Corps or Army Cadet Force.

PART I. I hereby certify that (Rank) Pte. (Name and initials) TOSELAND, C.E. RKFG/26/1 of .... Battery 5 (KD) Northants .... Regiment HOME GUARD has qualified Company .... Battalion in the Proficiency Badge tests as laid down in the pamphlet "Qualifications for, and Conditions governing the Award of the Home Guard Proficiency Badges and Certificates" for the following subjects:—

Subject	Date	Initials
1. General knowledge (all candidates)	17. 4. 44	
2. Rifle	3. 4. 44	
3. 36 M Grenade	3. 4. 44	
*4. (a) Other weapon Sten	12. 4. 44	
(b) Signalling		
*5. (a) Battlecraft, (b) Coast Artillery, (c) Heavy A.A. Bty. work, (d) "Z" A.A. Battery work, (e) Bomb Disposal, (f) Watermanship, (g) M.T.	17. 4. 44	
*6. (a) Map Reading, (b) Field works, (c) First Aid	24. 4. 44	

Date 3. 4. 1944   Signature .... * Resident or Member of the Board.

Date 17. 4. 1944   Signature .... * President or Member of the Board.

Date 24. 4. 1944   Signature .... * President or Member of the Board.

Date .... 194—   Signature .... * President or Member of the Board.

Date .... 194—   Signature .... * President or Member of the Board.

PART II. I certify that (Rank) Pte. (Name and initials) TOSELAND, C.E. RKFG/26/1 of .... Battery 5 (KD) Northants .... Regiment HOME GUARD, having duly passed Company .... Battalion the Proficiency tests in the subjects detailed above in accordance with the pamphlet and is hereby authorized to wear the Proficiency Badge as laid down in Regulations for the Home Guard, Vol. 1, 1942, para. 41d.

Date .... 194—   Signature .... LIEUT. COLONEL COMMANDING Commanding .....) 5. NORTHAMPTONSHIRE H.G. HOME G.

PART III. If the holder joins H.M. Forces, his Company or equivalent Commander will record below any particulars which he considers useful in assessing the man's value on arrival at the T.E., P.T.C., R.T.C., e.g. service, rank, duties on which employed, power of leadership, etc.

Date .... 194—   Signature .... O.C.

* Delete where not applicable.

Certificate of proficiency awarded to Cyril Toseland. These were presented in recognition of skills attained during service in the Home Guard.

1940 Four Toseland brothers from Warkton, Alfred, Archie, Cyril and Arthur, all of whom joined the Home Guard. These brothers were not conscripted into the armed forces because they were all employed in agriculture which was a designated reserved occupation. Both Alfred and Archie tried on numerous occasions to join the army but were refused permission to leave the land. Arthur did enlist into the army but was discharged on medical grounds, and Cyril was ineligible due to his age.

Warkton Home Guard platoon 1940 comprising sixteen members. In 1941 following the threat of invasion, additional farm workers from other villages were attached to Warkton Home Guard. Donovan Lane (in the centre) was the Captain, Alfred Toseland was sergeant, Cecil Clifford Corporal, Cyril Toseland and Albert Law Lance Corporals. At the Northamptonshire Home Guard shooting competition in 1943, held at Sywell, Alfred Toseland came first, Cecil Clifford second and Cyril Toseland third.

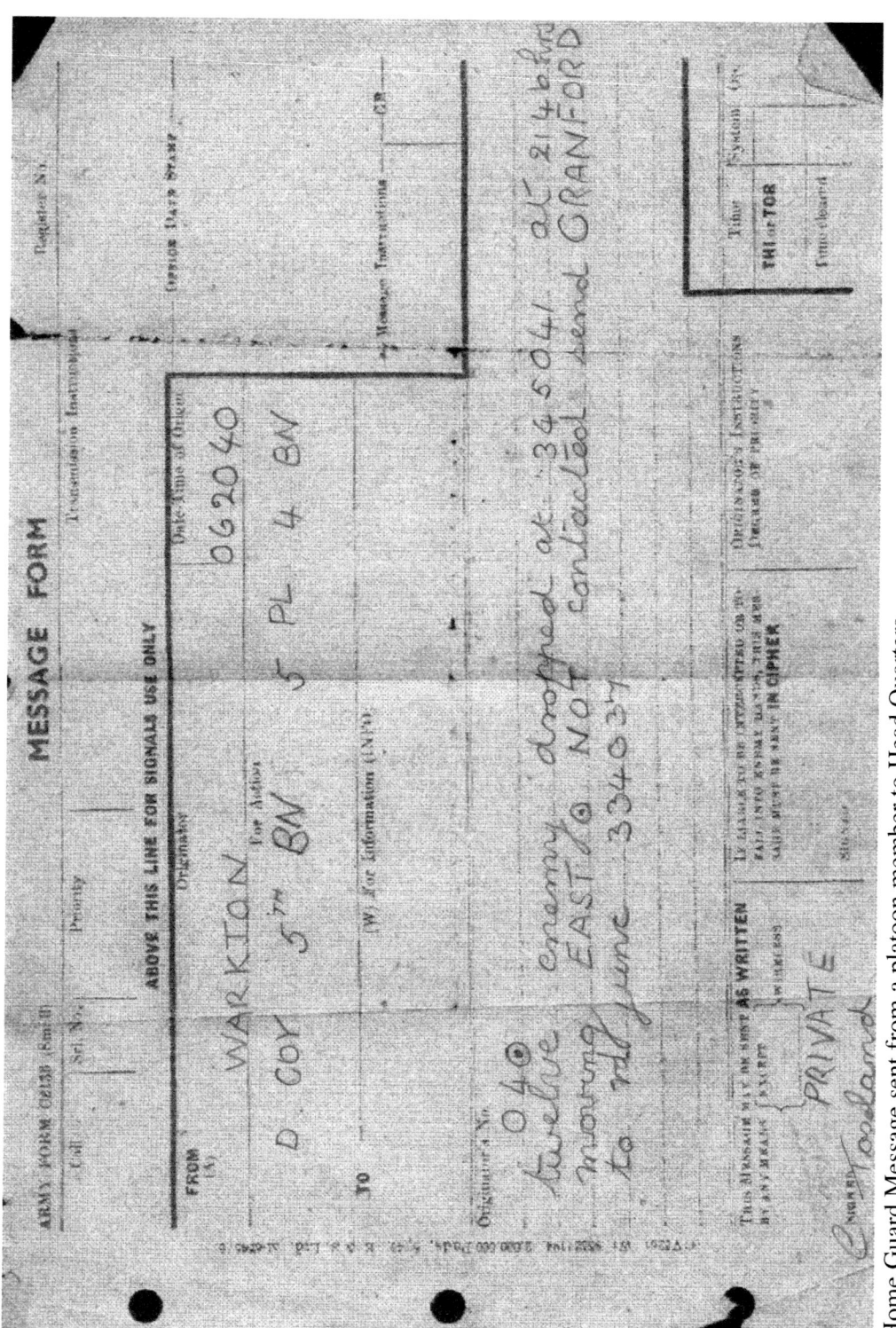

Home Guard Message sent from a platoon member to Head Quarters.

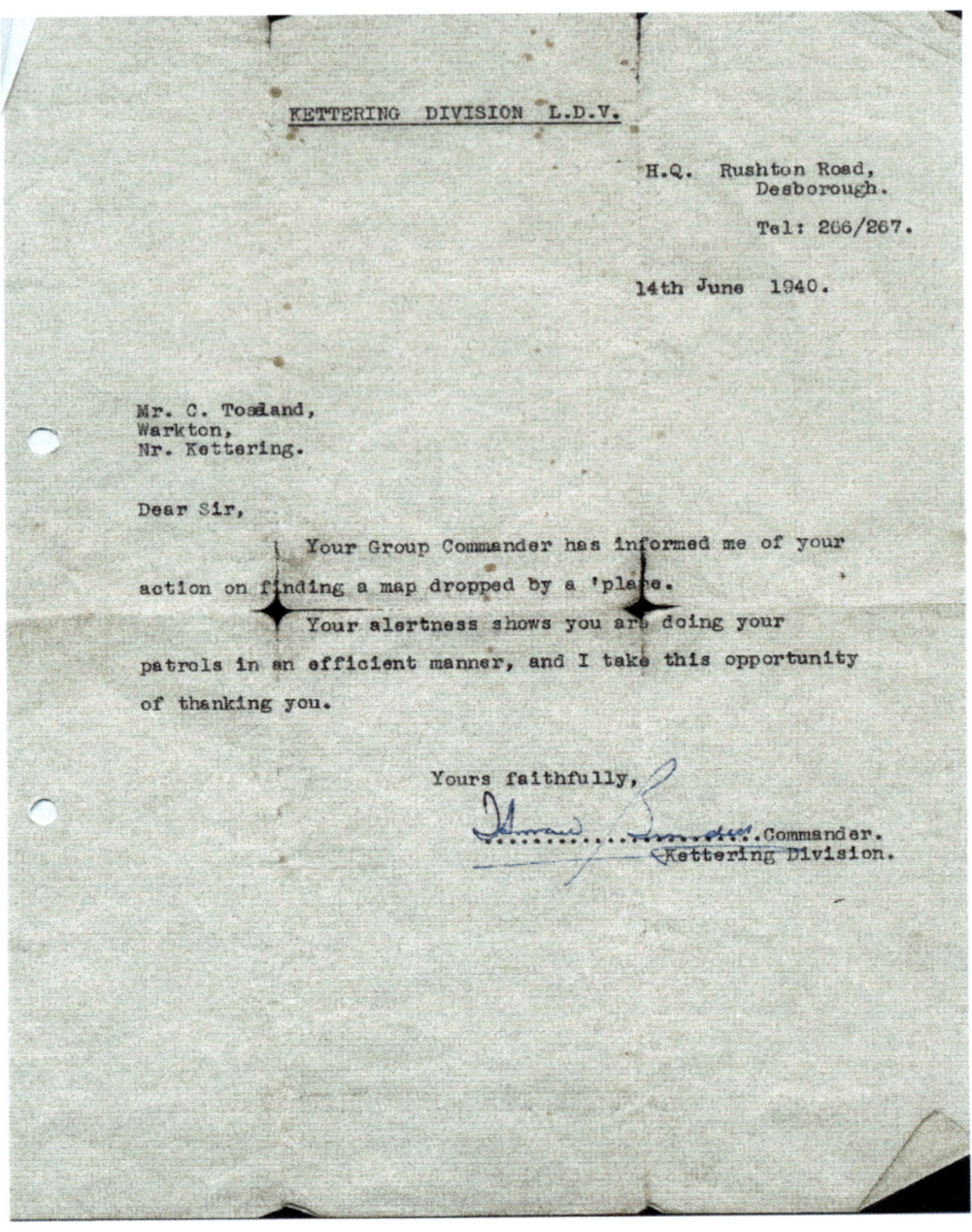

KETTERING DIVISION L.D.V.

H.Q. Rushton Road,
Desborough.

Tel: 266/267.

14th June 1940.

Mr. C. Toseland,
Warkton,
Nr. Kettering.

Dear Sir,

Your Group Commander has informed me of your
action on finding a map dropped by a 'plane.

Your alertness shows you are doing your
patrols in an efficient manner, and I take this opportunity
of thanking you.

Yours faithfully,

..........................Commander.
Kettering Division.

June 14th 1940 A letter sent to Cyril Toseland, in recognition of finding an important document that had fallen from an aircraft.

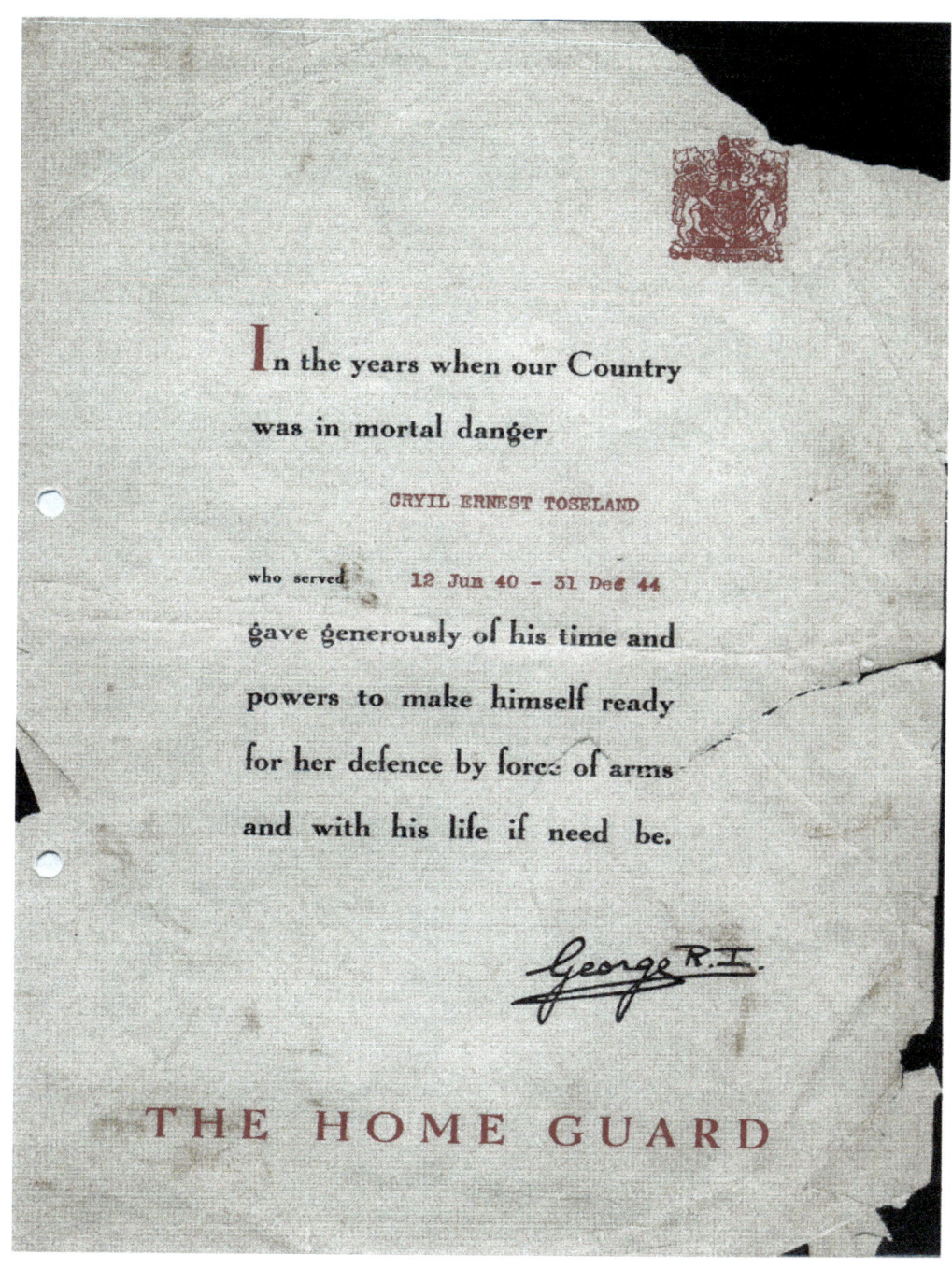

In the years when our Country

was in mortal danger

CRYIL ERNEST TOSELAND

who served   12 Jun 40 – 31 Dec 44

gave generously of his time and

powers to make himself ready

for her defence by force of arms

and with his life if need be.

George R.I.

THE HOME GUARD

A copy of a certificate of recognition for service in the Home Guard.

HOME GUARD. KETTERING BOROUGH BATTALION
"C" COMPANY.

= Church Parade =

at St. Edmund's, Warkton,

(By kind invitation of the Rev C. R. NORCOCK, M.A., Rector)

With the Kettering Rifle Band

SUNDAY, NOVEMBER 10TH, AT 11 A.M.

1944

HYMNS

1.   NATIONAL ANTHEM.

2. SOLDIERS OF CHRIST, ARISE.
(A. & M. 270)

SOLDIERS of Christ, arise,
   And put your armour on ;
Strong in the strength which God supplies,
   Through His Eternal Son.

Strong in the Lord of Hosts,
   And in His mighty power ;
Who in the strength of Jesus trusts
   Is more than conqueror.

Stand then in His great might,
   With all His strength endued ;
And take, to arm you for the fight,
   The panoply of God.

From strength to strength go on,
   Wrestle and fight, and pray ;
Tread all the powers of darkness down,
   And win the well-fought day.

That having all things done,
   And all your conflicts past,
Ye may obtain, through Christ alone,
   A crown of joy at last.

Jesu, Eternal Son,
   We praise Thee and adore,
Who art with God the Father One
   And Spirit evermore.

3. FIGHT THE GOOD FIGHT.
(A. & M. 540)

FIGHT the good fight, with all thy might,
   Christ is thy Strength, and Christ thy
Lay hold on life, and it shall be   [Right ;
Thy joy and crown eternally.

Run the straight race through God's good grace,
Lift up thine eyes, and seek His Face ;
Life with its way before us lies.
Christ is the path, and Christ the prize.

Cast care aside, lean on thy Guide ;
His boundless mercy will provide :
Trust, and thy trusting soul shall prove
Christ is its life, and Christ its love.

Faint not nor fear, His Arms are near,
He changeth not, and thou art dear ;
Only believe, and thou shalt see
That Christ is all in all to thee.

4. ONWARD, CHRISTIAN SOLDIERS.
(A. & M 391)

ONWARD, Christian soldiers
   Marching as to war,
With the Cross of Jesus
   Going on before.
Christ the Royal Master
   Leads against the foe ;
Forward into battle,
   See, His banners go !

   Onward, Christain soldiers,
      Marching as to war,
   With the Cross of Jesus
      Going on before.

At the sign of triumph
   Satan's host doth flee :
On then, Christian soldiers,
   On to victory.
Hell's foundations quiver
   At the shout of praise ;
Brothers, lift your voices,
   Loud your anthems raise.

      Onward, &c.

Like a mighty army
   Moves the Church of God ;
Brothers, we are treading
   Where the Saints have trod ;
We are not divided.
   All one body we.
One in hope and doctrine,
   One in charity.

      Onward, &c.

Crowns and thrones may perish.
   Kingdoms rise and wane,
But the Church of Jesus
   Constant will remain ;
Gates of hell can never
   'Gainst that Church prevail
We have Christ's own promise,
   And that cannot fail.

      Onward, &c.

Onward, then ye people,
   Join our happy throng,
Blend with ours your voices
   In the triumph song ;
Glory, laud, and honour
   Unto Christ the King,
This through countless ages
   Men and Angels sing.

      Onward, &c.

(left)

Service sheet printed for St Edmunds Church Warkton on the occasion of the disbandment of the Home Guard on Remembrance Sunday in 1944. This is the only time in living memory that the church was overflowing with people to such an extent that many had to listen to the Thanksgiving Service from the churchyard. On VE Day 8th May 1945 a large bonfire with an effigy of Hitler on the top was lit and the veterans of the Home Guard used all their left over thunder flashes and flares to celebrate the ending of the war in Europe. The whole village turned out to watch the proceedings. To celebrate victory in Japan on 12 August 1945, another bonfire was lit but there was no extra excitement caused by flares as these had all been let off in the May celebration.

Alec Bagshaw conscripted into the Royal Navy in 1942. When demobbed, he returned to his former employment as a carpenter at Boughton House. He is seen here with Brenda Toseland.

Fred Lumbers in 1942. He was transferred from the Home Guard to the Special Constabulary, his duties involved patrolling the Warkton area.

Fred Lumber's Constabulary Record.

NORTHAMPTONSHIRE CONSTABULARY.

Certificate of Service

DURING THE WAR 1939-1945.

The members of the Standing Joint Committee wish to show their warm appreciation of and thanks to

Special Constable Frederick Lumbers

for his valuable and loyal service to the County during the War Period.

Kenneth Murchison Chairman.

R. H.D. Bolton. Chief Constable.

Harry Eastbrook 1940. ARP warden "put that light out" one of the two wardens
for Warkton. The other warden was George Turner. All homes had to cover their
windows with blackout curtains during the hours of darkness. This was obligatory
until VE day. No bonfires were permitted after dark, and vehicles had their lights
adapted to ensure that the beams only covered the roadway immediately in front.

Should they be required the following implements, tools
and other articles necessary for the occasion may be found at :-

PICKS SHOVELS BARROWS LADDERS

Mr.Eastbrook,	Mr.Geo.Turner
Mr.T.A.Turner,	Mr.Hay
Mr.Bliss,	Mr.Sargeant
Mr.Lane,	Mr.Lomas
Mr.Palmer at Warkton Lodge.	

CARS   Mr.Hay, Mr.Lomas, Mr.Lamb, Mr.Lane.

LORRIES   Mr.Geo.Toseland.   Mr.Palmer

TRACTORS   Mr.Hay, Mr.Lomas, Mr.Turner.

HORSES AND CARTS   Mr.Hay   Mr.Lomas Mr.Turner   Mr.Sargeant
                     Mr.Toseland.   Mr.Palmer

STIRRUP PUMPS   Mr.Eastbrook, Mr.Geo Turner, Mr.T.Turner,
                  Mr.Lane   Mr.Lamb   Mr.CecilClifford,
                  Mr.Bagshaw,   Mr.Bliss   Mr.Lomas
                  Mr.Saunders (Oneacre) and at the Church.
                  Mr.Palmer, Mr.Hay and Mr.Toseland.

THE FIRST AID POST   is at Mrs.Lane's.

And ORDINARY GARDENING TOOLS, such as spades, forks, rakes etc
                  may be found at practically every cottage in
                  the village.

A notice issued by the local authority, informing the village of equipment that they
may require in the event of an emergency. These notices were given to every
household in the village and posted on notice boards.

NORTHAMPTONSHIRE COUNTY COUNCIL. **SECRET.**

Tel. No. 4311.

I.C.No.17.

County Hall,
Guildhall Road,
Northampton.

4 MAR 1945

Dear Sir,

Invasion Committees.

As there appears to be considerable doubt among Invasion Committees as to which villages are to be "defended places" in t event of invasion, I have obtained a list of the towns and villa concerned from the Sub-Area Commander.

I am now able to inform you that your village is to be a "defended place". This means that Home Guard elements will not be withdrawn from your village but at which Home Guard units in outlying villages may be concentrated.

It is important, therefore, that you should complete your combined defence scheme in conjunction with your local Military Commander as soon as possible.

Yours faithfully,

hiHGage

County Invasion Officer.

To the Chairmen of Invasion Committees in Rural Districts.
(whose villages are "defended places").

C.Lamb, Esq.,
The Old Rectory,
Warkton.

A secret letter sent to Mr Charles Lamb, Chairman of the Warkton Invasion Committee. He also served as Chairman of the Military Service (hardship) Committee under the National Service Armed Forces Act.

Alan Toseland on "Credit Note" in the Royal Army Veterinary Corps, Melton Mowbray, in 1954 during National Service, which continued until 1960. The 2 other Warkton boys who were called up for National Service, after the war, were Richard Bussey and David Issitt both of these boys served in the RAF

German Prisoners of War (POWs) were brought to Boughton Park in June 1944, they took over the camp that the American troops had vacated when they left to fight in operation "Overlord" in 1944. There were about 2,000 POWs held there, and many of them were bussed out daily to work either on the Estate or local farms.

Most farms had at least 1 prisoner working for them on a regular basis, but at hay time and harvest, many more were employed. These were ordinary troops and were trusted not to escape. The SS Soldiers were kept in a separate wired off area and were only allowed out under armed guard.

These POWs were repatriated in 1947, but as a lot of them would have been returning to the Russian Zone in Germany, a number of them took their own lives instead of having to face the suffering that they knew would face them. Some of them stayed in England, and obtained employment, starting families having married into English families.

In 1946, when a lot of British Servicemen were being demobbed and returned to their previous places of work, there was not enough work for the POWs, especially in the winter time. A large number of POWs from Boughton Camp were employed to restore all the gravel paths in Boughton Park and beyond. Apparently in the 1850s, there was a gang of men solely employed to keep these paths in good order. But in 1946, according to the villagers, these paths and bridleways had not been maintained in living memory. When the POWs had completed this work, everything looked magnificent with not a weed in sight.

A view of Warkton looking east from the Stamford Road in September 2000. In the centre of this photograph it is possible to see the recent extensions to St Edmunds Church on either side of the tower.